HISTORY FILES   The Slave Trade

AM I NOT A MAN AND A BROTHER?

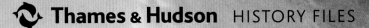

Thames & Hudson HISTORY FILES

The Slave Trade

JAMES WALVIN

HALF-TITLE 'Am I not a man and a
brother?' Woodcut illustration from an
1837 American broadside publication of
John Greenleaf Whittier's antislavery
poem, 'Our Countrymen in Chains'.
TITLE PAGES European cruelty, the
destruction of family life and African
despair: all the ingredients of a romantic
view of enslavement on the African
coast, c. 1820.
THIS PAGE Log entries from the slave ship
Molly (1759). Unusually, this one lists
the Africans by name, not number.

First published in 2011 in paperback in
the United States of America by
Thames & Hudson Inc., 500 Fifth
Avenue, New York, New York 10110

thamesandhudsonusa.com

Library of Congress Catalog Card
Number 2010936807

ISBN 978-0-500-28917-4

Printed in China through Asia Pacific
Offset Ltd

Contents

Europe supported by Africa & America.

Blake Sculp.^t

Introduction

A Trade with Global Consequences

The Atlantic slave trade was one of the most extraordinary movements of people in world history. Between around 1500 and the 1860s about 12 million Africans were loaded on to Atlantic slave ships; of these, some 11 million survived (though many barely) to reach landfall in the Americas. Yet until quite recently the full significance of this massive enforced displacement of humanity was largely overlooked by historians. Just a generation ago, the slave trade was considered to be of interest only to maritime historians, or to those studying the histories of Africa or the Americas. Today, the story of the Atlantic slave trade is accepted as central to the history of three continents – Africa, the Americas and Europe – with implications for the entire world.

OPPOSITE 'Europe Supported by Africa & America', William Blake's engraving of the symbolic link between Africa, Europe and the Americas, published in 1796.

For nearly four centuries, the Atlantic slave ships linked the peoples and economic fortunes of utterly different and geographically separated communities. Huge volumes of European goods were ferried to West Africa, where they were exchanged for Africans who were then forcibly transported (the so-called Middle Passage) to work the fertile lands of the Americas, cultivating crops – notably sugar, rice, tobacco and cotton – which were exported back as the luxuries and then the essentials of the wider world. In the process, the Atlantic slave trade became a global economic system, sucking in goods from ever more distant corners of the globe

Africans were bartered for a range of imported goods. These 17th- and early 18th-century Italian glass beads were exported from Bristol, bound for the slave coast of Africa.

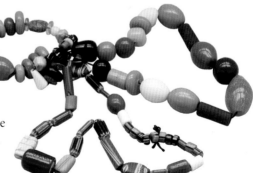

Elmina ('The Mine'), c. 1502. The Portuguese headquarters on the coast was intended initially to safeguard the trade in gold – and later the trade in slaves.

OPPOSITE Illustration by Capt. Samuel Gamble from the logbook of the slave ship *Sandown*, showing enslaved Africans being marched to the coast of Sierra Leone, 1793.

and supplying far-flung markets. Tea from China, coffee from Arabia, chocolate from Mexico (mixed with slave-grown sugar) – all these commodities and more were soon inextricably linked in a network of trade and consumption. And all was made possible, initially at least, by the sweat of Africans toiling on the plantations of the Americas.

To outsiders it seemed that 'Africa' (a concept known to Europeans, though not to Africans) was a cornucopia capable of delivering endless supplies of labour to European and American traders. Millions of African slaves were taken from a slaving coast that stretched thousands of miles, from Sene-Gambia south to Angola, and even round the Cape and on to Mozambique. However, the great bulk of those enslaved were drawn from the much narrower geography of western Central Africa. They came originally from regions in the interior and were usually seized violently, in war or in raids, by African traders and hostile communities who were well aware of the European merchants waiting on the coast. A majority of the Africans bundled on to the ships were male (by the last years of the trade, in the mid-19th century, most were male children).

In the popular mind this trade was triangular, but in reality its geography was much more complex. In addition, we can now see two distinct slave trades: one serving the North Atlantic (providing Africans for the Caribbean and North America), the other in the South Atlantic, serving Brazil. And cutting across all these were other movements of ships and trade: vessels sailing to and from Europe

Representation of a Lott of Fullom's bringing their Slaves for Sale to the Europeans. which generally commences anually in December, or early in January, being prevented from comeing down sooner by the rivers being overflowed and their paths impassable, from the heavy rains which end in November. they sometimes come upwards of one thousand Miles out of the interior parts of the Country are Arm'd with Bows Arrows & Spears, one quiver of Arrows the early are poison'd to defend themselves with, another not so which they hunt with and are very dextrous seldom missing their game. the Slaves they make fast round the Neck along stick which is secured round the others neck from one to another so that one Man can stop fifty and stops them at his pleasure at Night their hands are tyed behind their backs.

Sugar, from the cane fields to the finished product: a series of 19th-century French engravings show harvesting, crushing, boiling and processing cane sugar.

and Africa, ships travelling direct from North America to Africa and back, and large numbers of ships crossing back and forth from Brazil to Africa. This complex and confusing flow of goods and people shaped Atlantic trade for centuries.

If there was one engine driving the slave trade, it was sugar. Wherever sugar cane could be grown, Africans were considered vital and were imported in increasing numbers. The majority were taken to Brazil, with the next largest proportion going to the Caribbean islands. Far fewer Africans were shipped to North America, where they worked first in tobacco, then in rice and finally in cotton.

The key to successful slave labour was the plantation, which provided the structure for disciplining workers to submit to the unrelenting grind of cultivating labour-intensive crops in harsh conditions. Indeed, Africans and plantations went hand in hand, producing tropical staples for Western consumption and profit.

As societies matured across the Americas, Africans and their local-born descendants were soon to be found in all walks of life: from sailors (even on the slave ships) to miners and to cowboys on the American frontiers. Africans spread throughout the Americas, developing their own communities in European colonial cities. Slavery soon seeped out of the plantations, and in many places African slaves worked side by side with free and indentured labourers. However, the overwhelming majority of enslaved Africans were transported specifically to work on plantations.

But why were the Africans enslaved? After all, European countries had by this time largely abandoned their traditional attachment to unfree labour at home. Yet just when they had turned their backs on slavery at home, Europeans came to think of African slaves as the ideal solution to the labour needs of their distant colonies. Africans were apparently cheap, easily recruited (and equally easily replaced) and seemed to meet all the requirements of the European planters of the Americas.

Each of the 11 million Africans who survived the Atlantic crossing was marked by what happened on the slave ships. It was a uniquely horrifying experience, which left deep scars on African communities across the Americas. The ordeals of violent seizure, captivity in the slave holds and the traumas of the prolonged Atlantic crossing were the fate and would become the memory of millions of

Africans. Whatever their individual African origin or their final American destination (often far from first landfall), Africans were profoundly affected by the terrible circumstances of their capture and transportation.

By the time the slave trade ended in the 1860s there had been some 40,000 slave voyages. Although the British did not initiate the trade, they perfected it, and by the time they abolished their own trade in 1807, they had carried more than 3 million Africans across the Atlantic. But all the European maritime powers, from Portugal to Brandenburg in eastern Germany, were actively involved. Major cities including London, Bristol and pre-eminently Liverpool in Britain, Bordeaux in France and Lisbon in Portugal all prospered from the trade, and ships were also dispatched to the West African slave coast from smaller ports such as Honfleur in France.

The slave trade was much more than simply a new form of international commercial transaction. In the tortuous and complex process of enslavement and transportation, the African was reduced from a human being to an item of trade: to be bought, sold and haggled over like any other commodity. Nor was this transformation

The French port of Bordeaux, 1759: elegant and prosperous, at the height of its slave trading fortunes.

Traditional slave trading in Arabia: African slaves and Arab merchants in the market in Yemen, 13th century.

of the African into an object simply a matter of economic practice. Across the colonial Americas and in Europe, legislation and treaties established that Africans be treated as things. In the 18th century, for example, the British Parliament passed dozens of Acts that defined the African as a commodity. Europeans and Americans quickly became accustomed to viewing the African as a chattel: a valuable article with a price attached.

Of course, this enforced removal of African people began long before the arrival of the European ships: there had been a thriving overland Arab slave trade for centuries. The result was that, for around a millennium, sub-Saharan Africa suffered a massive loss of population, generally the fittest and youngest, causing widespread and incalculable human and social as well as economic damage.

The slave trade also had a huge impact on the Americas and Europe, but in very different ways. In the Americas the most obvious consequence was demographic growth and transformation. Areas that had once been only lightly populated by indigenous peoples became effectively African: although technically European colonies, they were in fact African settlements on the far side of the Atlantic. The slave trade even affected the landscape. The labour of enslaved Africans converted Caribbean islands, for example, into major agri-cultural–industrial regions, their skylines dotted with windmills and factory chimneys, as raw sugar cane was transformed into crude sugar. In the process, a new visual imagery also emerged, of orderly tropical agriculture, its produce dispatched through new towns and ports (Bridgetown in Barbados was the busiest port in the entire English-speaking Americas until 1700). These colonial settlements were connected to Africa and Europe by the regular arrival and departure of growing numbers of ships criss-crossing the Atlantic. They arrived in the Americas with Africans and material for the plan-tations, and departed with slave-grown produce.

For Europe (and indeed the wider world) the consequences of all this were also enormous, although some were more obvious than others. The rapid development of towns and ports involved in

This marble statue of an African boy was displayed to advertise the offices of a local slave trader in the French port of Nantes in the early 18th century.

The urban and social prosperity that flowed from the slave trade are evident in this 19th-century engraving of the theatre in Nantes.

19th-century Cuban sugar plantation, where slaves work in the fields while the factory processes the raw sugar.

slaving was one visible effect of the trade. Profits from both the ships and the plantations flowed back to Europe to be invested in docks, quaysides, port facilities and related industries as well as fashionable rural retreats for those who prospered. Glasgow and Liverpool, Nantes and Bordeaux – all were transformed by their involvement in the Atlantic slave trade. The elegant homes of slave merchants and returned planters were echoed by impressive warehouses, banks and the offices of insurance and shipping companies, changing the urban landscape of 18th-century Europe and America.

Further ramifications included the expansion of international finance, in the form of bills of credit, which arose directly from the Atlantic slave empires. Major industries, notably ship-building with all its vital ancillaries (rope-making, sail-making, armaments, victualling, gun-making and metal industries for the chains and manacles), were spawned or stimulated by the slave trade. Plantations throughout the Americas devoured imported European goods by the boatload. Coal from European mines found its way to the Caribbean plantations to fuel the processing of sugar. Agricultural equipment, seeds and plants, leather goods for the cattle and horses, whips to marshal and chastise the workers – all crossed the Atlantic to sustain the plantations. Planters' tables were laden with imported goods, from cutlery to glassware, French wine and brandy (drinks that also found favour on the African coast in the barter for slaves). Salted cod from the Newfoundland fisheries became a major food for Caribbean slaves, and by the end of the 18th century they were also eating breadfruit and planting a new strain of sugar cane, both brought from Tahiti. North American trees were used for building the slave ships and for the shingles on Caribbean buildings. Some West African slave forts were constructed from millions of bricks shipped from Europe to Africa as ballast.

Here, then, was an Atlantic economy, based on African slavery, with almost incalculable reach and influence. Thousands of ships from a host of European (and, later, American) maritime nations trawled along an extensive stretch of African coast for human cargoes. Huge numbers of Africans simply did not survive the Atlantic crossing, succumbing to maltreatment and a range of ail-

The meticulous bookkeeping of the slave trade is evident in the entries for enslaved Africans in the accounts of the slave ship *Molly*, 1759.

The importance of the West Indian trade to London is shown in this elevated view of the new West India Docks under construction, 1804.

ments contracted in the prolonged process of enslavement in Africa and during their seaborne imprisonment. Nonetheless, the very great majority of enslaved Africans survived the ships and landed in the Americas.

Today, few would dispute that the slave trade was an exceptionally cruel and brutal system, both inhumane and immoral. Yet very few contemporaries viewed it that way. A conundrum is that many of the leading participants in this historical drama regarded themselves as devout Christians, God-fearing men who supported their local churches and gave thanks to the Almighty for their successful business in Atlantic slavery. We know of many devout slave captains, religious slave merchants and pious planters. There were, it is true, objectors to the entire slave system, critics who took moral and religious offence at the very concept of slavery. They, however, were few and far between throughout the history of Atlantic slavery. Change began to come, slowly, from the mid-18th century, when the slave trade was at its height. But until then, the voice of ethical outrage was barely audible above the sound of profitable commerce and trade.

The business of the slave trade – the noisy confusion of docksides crowded with vessels fresh from, or destined for, Africa, the Caribbean or the Americas – simply drowned out any dissenting voices. Who heeded a few outraged individuals when the slave trade yielded such obvious bounty?

The victims had, of course, always struggled against their fate. The enslaved Africans, cooped up in appalling conditions, posed an ever-present threat to every slave ship. But the sense among Europeans and Americans that the slave system itself was morally flawed and irreligious – indeed, that it was unchristian – was a very late development. Then, quite suddenly, small groups of Europeans and North Americans began to turn against the entrenched and lucrative business of slave trading. Having perfected the profitable transportation of millions of Africans across the Atlantic, the maritime nations of Europe and North America (led by the Danes, the British and the Americans) finally began, in the early 1800s, legislating to ban the slave trade.

After passing their own acts of abolition, the British and Americans embarked on a crusade to persuade, or force, everyone else to follow their example and outlaw the slave trade. Despite their efforts, over 2.5 million additional Africans were transported across the

The indefatigable foot soldier of the abolition movement: Thomas Clarkson, in old age, addressing the first Anti-Slavery Society Convention in 1840.

Generally Africans were depicted in the holds of slave ships as in this 1843 French engraving: the effect is excessively neat and orderly.

Atlantic as slaves in the following decades. Moreover, the institution of slavery itself lived on: in the British colonies until 1838, in French possessions until 1848 and in the United States until 1865; it was not abolished in Brazil until 1888.

Nevertheless, in the 19th century the Western world turned its back on the slave trade and slavery. Did this complete reversal of European and American practice over the previous three centuries represent a new moral dawn, a revulsion against outdated customs? Or did it reflect deeper, more fundamental economic changes: was slavery no longer economically viable? Perhaps it was an amalgam of the two. Perhaps new, more profitable means of production and resources of labour – free labour – coincided with a changed world outlook and morality in the West.

Whatever the explanation (and historians continue to debate

the issue), the end of the slave trade marked a dramatic turnabout. The system which had served Europeans so well in their settlement and development of key areas of the Americas and brought them such material reward was rejected. More than that, the West came to view slavery as a moral aberration. Indeed, Europeans and Americans became fierce enemies of slavery and slave trading, anxious to destroy it wherever they encountered it in Africa, India and Asia. Ending slavery became part of a new global moral crusade: one of the progressive civilizing gifts the West could bring to benighted and backward parts of the world. It was as if the West's own slaving past had never existed. But if Europeans did need to be reminded of that past, they had only to glance at the surviving built environment from the 18th century, or to look at the descendants of African slaves scattered throughout the Americas and Europe. For these and many other people, the history of slavery and the Atlantic slave trade continued to hold a poignancy and relevance even if others had forgotten. And it is a sobering thought that there are an estimated 20 million slaves on earth today.

African children rescued from modern-day trafficking at the border between Burkina Faso and Ivory Coast, 2008. They were being sent to work on cocoa plantations. In 2007, 269 child victims of slavery were intercepted and rescued in one province alone.

Chapter 1

The European Slave Trade with Africa

OPPOSITE European maritime
adventurers explore the wider
world. The *Livro das Armadas*
describes Vasco da Gama's
1502 expedition to the Indies:
his ship is depicted in the
centre of the page.

Africa lies at the heart of this book. Its enormous land mass, thousands of miles of Atlantic coastline, complex riverine systems and, above all, its people form the core of much of what follows. Africans and Europeans were known to each other long before the arrival of European ships off the West African coast in the 15th century. Africans had been seen in Europe for centuries. They often arrived from North Africa across the Mediterranean as slaves brought from the interior via overland trade routes, mainly across the Sahara and along the Nile. But by and large sub-Saharan Africa remained *terra incognita* until the 'Age of Exploration' initiated by the Portuguese in the 15th century.

A Portuguese merchant
(far right) trades for Africans
and ivory in Sierra Leone, 1682.

Tornou á India Dom Vasq da gama Almirante por capitão mór, e partio a dez de feuᵉ co
vinte vellas. Repartidas em tres capitanias - S. Vicente sodree tio delle dom vasquo da
gama Irmão de sua may q leuaua a sucessão por capitão mór de cinq vellas que a vião de
figar na India em fauor das feytorias de cochi e, cananor, e tambem pera e algũs mes-
ses do verão srem guardar a boca do estreyto do mar Roxo, e a capitania mór doutras
cinq vellas que não estauão prestes se deu a esteuão da gama primo co Irmão de Vasquo
da gama, que de pois partio a primeyro dabril; na qual frota hião estes capitaᵉs

S. pantalião

Pedrafonsso daguiar

Diogo frz correa
por feytor de corsim

Lionarda

Dom luis coutinᵍ S ramiro

S. Jeronimo

Dom vasq da gama

S. grauiel

gil matoso

João lopez peresthello

bate cabello

Ruy de castanheda

gil frz

leytua noua

Francisq dacunha
das Ilhas terceyras

Antonio do campo
com temporal esgarrou e
mes perdido foy tmd naᵉ
e hiua q Ilhas na costa de
Melinde sem saber onde es-
taua

Africa was a fabled land of valuable commodities, notably gold and spices, that were much prized by Europeans. Until the 15th century, however, the Atlantic coast of Africa remained inaccessible and sea voyages effectively ended at Cape Bojador, south of the Canaries. Powerful currents would carry ships further south but also prevented their return, although some Europeans had indeed sailed south, and a few had even made the perilous trip back overland to the Mediterranean.

The situation changed in the 15th century, thanks to a string of remarkable transformations in Europe itself. Innovative ship-building, navigational improvements and the gradual development of modern cartography were all stimulated by a commercial and political determination to explore ever further south along the African coast. These explorations were inspired in large part by Prince Henry the Navigator of Portugal. But they were also driven by a desire to outflank the dominance of Islam, which had cut off Europe's tradi-

The pioneering Portuguese along the coast of Africa, in a map of the world, 1489.

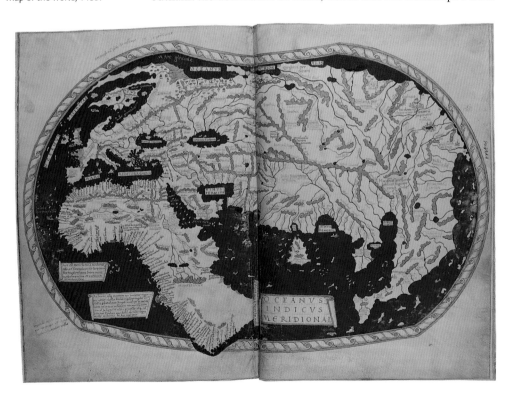

Henry's importance has often been exaggerated, but it is widely accepted that his leadership of an expansive commercial and maritime nation was critical in opening West Africa to European exploration and trade. Henry was keen to capitalize on what was known of Africa's fabled wealth – and perhaps to make contact with the fabled Christian kingdom of Prester John, thought to lie deep in the heart of Africa. The Pope also authorized and strengthened Henry's determination to take a more aggressive role in the effort to outflank Islam, for which the only means possible was by sea. In 1415 the capture of Ceuta, an ancient North African port city on the Strait of Gibraltar, first revealed the variety and richness of trade flowing from sub-Saharan Africa. Above all, it was the gold carried along the overland caravan routes that caught the attention of the Portuguese: sailing to West Africa would enable Portugal to tap into that most valued of all African commodities. Backed by Henry's studious prompting and encouragement, successive expeditions pushed ever further south into the Atlantic. By the time of his death, the Portuguese had settled the Atlantic islands of Madeira (1420), the Azores (1427) and the Cape Verde Islands (1456–60), and Portuguese ships had reached Sierra Leone. They were trading on the African coast – and had shipped perhaps a thousand Africans as slaves.

Prince Henry the Navigator, whose support was one of the powerful forces behind the Portuguese urge to overseas exploration and empire.

tional overland links through the eastern Mediterranean to the exotic goods of Asia. The Portuguese pioneered a series of daring ventures along the African coast: by 1444 they had reached Senegal, and by 1488 they had rounded the southern tip of the continent at the Cape of Good Hope. The whole of the West African coastline was now exposed to European maritime incursions.

As they moved slowly south after 1415, Europeans encountered African coastal societies linked to complex states and trading systems inland. These largely followed the routes carved by the massive river systems, from the Senegal to the Congo, bringing people and goods from the African interior to the Atlantic coast. There were also African coastal trades that linked one region to another. Thus, as European explorers and traders cautiously nosed their way south along the Atlantic coast, they encountered a myriad of people, complex and far-flung trading systems and a variety of states. Most

appealing of all, they encountered an array of attractive commodities. Among these were Africans traded as slaves.

Africa was home to many forms of slavery and slave trading. Slavery was rooted in Islamic Africa (which stretched deep into the continent) and was basic to a number of societies in sub-Saharan Africa. Indeed, slaves were the principal form of capital south of the Sahara. Unsurprisingly, Europeans began to make use of the slave trading systems they encountered on the Atlantic coast.

Initially, the Portuguese traded African slaves between different African societies, in effect becoming middlemen in the movement of people from one African coastal region to another. By the end of the 15th century the Portuguese had established a thriving business in Kongo (whose rulers also accepted Christianity), shipping African slaves from there to the new sugar plantations on the islands of Sao Tome and Principe in the Gulf of Guinea. They also sent African slaves back to Portugal. These activities evolved before Europeans began to develop slave plantations in the Americas.

At first Europeans were looking only for immediate profits from trade on the African coast, and they pursued this through raids and seizures. But, led by the Portuguese Crown, they soon appreciated

We selected those slaves to be made into soldiers and a channel for Islam, because…they are a race who give little trouble,…accepting things as they find them….

Ahmad al-Mansur, on recruiting black slaves for the Moroccan army, 16th century[1]

ABOVE An African view of Europeans, as portrayed in a 16th-century carved ivory salt-cellar from Benin.

OPPOSITE Portuguese map of western Europe and northwest Africa, 1563, showing the extent of Portuguese exploration and trade along the West African coastline.

that more lucrative commerce could be gained from a more settled and organized trade, notably for gold and pepper. The rewards could be lavish for the early private investors and adventurers, and in 1482 the Portuguese Crown began to sponsor its own expeditions – followed, much later, by other European monarchs keen to augment their coffers with the profits of the trade with West Africa. Thus, from an early date, the commercial appeal of Africa attracted both private and royal investment.

The expansion of profitable trade to Africa and beyond was made possible by gradual improvements in seafaring as well as the knowledge acquired from step-by-step explorations. The spices of

Kongo

When the Portuguese first sailed up the Congo River in 1483, they encountered the thriving commercial Kingdom of Kongo. It was rich in agricultural products and had access to metal goods and textiles – and slaves. Establishing a trading post and Christian missionaries, the Portuguese won over the local king and his elite to Christianity. Known (after 1506) as Alfonso I, the African monarch proved an avid convert, sending his nobles to Portugal for education and encouraging the spread of Christianity among his subjects. With the help of imported firearms and mercenaries, Alfonso was able to extend his influence, in return providing the Portuguese with regular supplies of slaves.

These were especially useful for the new Portuguese sugar plantations on the island of Sao Tome in the Gulf of Guinea, the major source of European sugar in the early 16th century. Although Alfonso later complained of the damage caused by the growing volume of often indiscriminate slave trading, he was too late to arrest the process. The basis was laid for the remarkably durable Portuguese involvement both in the region which became known as Angola and with an Atlantic slave-trading system that was to survive into the late 19th century.

The Portuguese made early conversions to Christianity in the Kingdom of Kongo, illustrated by this 17th-century crucifix from the region.

Benin bronze plaque depicting a local trader: his staff shows his rank. He also holds a manilla, the local currency.

India and, above all, the gold of West Africa were a seductive spur, encouraging pioneers from most of Europe's maritime powers to overcome the enormous dangers and difficulties of sailing south and along the African coastline. From the beginning the sailors in the Atlantic were a remarkably polyglot assortment, and this only increased as more ships came from Portugal, Spain, Holland, England, France and Germany. As this African trade grew, the Atlantic islands, especially the Canaries, became important staging posts for further ventures south along the African coast. Gradually, too, the initial predatory nature of the trade – characterized by attacks, raids and seizures of goods and people – was replaced by more orderly ('normal') commercial arrangements. Europeans quickly learned that African slaves could be employed both as items of trade and for labour in the Atlantic islands.

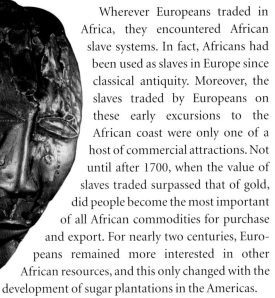

Precious objects from the kingdom of Asante, where power and influence were based on gold and later enhanced by slavery. These items were probably seized in the British attack on Kumasi in 1874.

Wherever Europeans traded in Africa, they encountered African slave systems. In fact, Africans had been used as slaves in Europe since classical antiquity. Moreover, the slaves traded by Europeans on these early excursions to the African coast were only one of a host of commercial attractions. Not until after 1700, when the value of slaves traded surpassed that of gold, did people become the most important of all African commodities for purchase and export. For nearly two centuries, Europeans remained more interested in other African resources, and this only changed with the development of sugar plantations in the Americas.

When European sailors began to explore the continent, however tentatively, West Africa was sparsely populated (ironic, considering the vast numbers of people subsequently removed for transportation to the Americas). More significant, perhaps, was its ferocious disease environment, which kept local populations in check and played havoc with the relatively few Europeans who tried to live along the African coast. Death and sickness became a regular litany both on shore and on board the growing numbers of European ships waiting at anchor off the coast. Indeed, the epidemiological problems of the region would compound the sufferings of Africans caught up in Atlantic slave trading throughout its history.

The development of sugar plantations in the new colonies of the Americas sparked a massive increase in the demand for slaves from the African coast. This utterly transformed the existing slavery practices within Africa itself by generating fierce searches for victims. The overwhelming majority of the millions who found themselves cast into the bellies of the Atlantic slave ships were initially acquired through violent means.

When the Portuguese built their first coastal forts – beginning in 1482 with Elmina Castle (Sao Jorge da Mina, St George of the Mine), in modern Ghana – these were designed not to incarcerate

Chanoine despaigne

A 16th-century priest accompanied by a Spanish serving boy (left) and a black slave (right), shackles attached to his ankles.

Silver ankle-ring from Asante, which seems to be modelled on slave shackles.

African slaves but to protect the gold brought out from the interior before it was loaded on to ships. European maritime nations built more than thirty forts along this stretch of the 'Gold Coast', and occasionally these would change hands as one power was superseded by another. Over time, Elmina and the other trading forts and military bases were used as 'factories' to house African slaves awaiting transfer to the Atlantic slave ships. They are a physical reminder and have thus come to symbolize the very nature of the European slaving presence on the coast of West Africa, despite the fact that most enslaved Africans acquired by Europeans were not actually housed in such forts.

I punish them with every sort of hardship until I compel them to behave as slaves.

Xenophon, Greek soldier and philosopher, 4th century BC[2]

The European pioneers of exploration and speculative trade revealed Africa as a source of lucrative commerce in precious commodities that were much prized in Europe. They also exposed Africa

European portrayal of buying Africans at the infamous slaving court of the King of Dahomey, 1793.

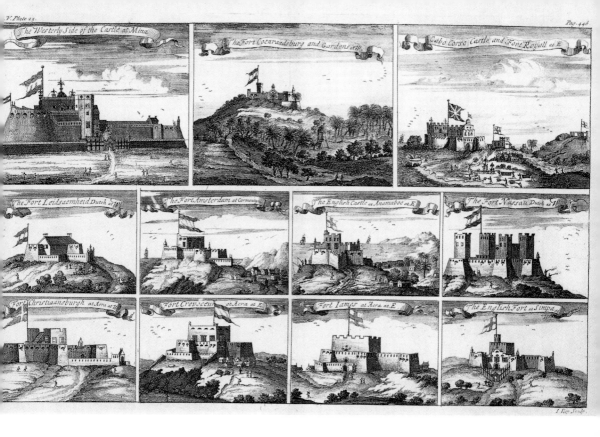

as an abundant supplier of slaves and showed that enslaved people could be purchased and then resold at any number of sites along the African coast, in the Atlantic islands, or even in Spain and Portugal. This was the origin of the subsequent mass transportation of unprecedented numbers of Africans into transatlantic slavery.

Europeans neither invented nor created African slavery, which they found thriving in various forms as they moved along the African coastline in the 15th century. However, the entire concept and scale were transformed from the 1540s when the new sugar plantations of Brazil began to encourage a qualitatively and quantitatively different form of slave trading: the long-distance oceanic trade across the Atlantic.

Forts on the West African Gold Coast (mainly in modern Ghana), built and controlled by the prominent European maritime powers, c. 1700.

Chapter 2

Sugar and Slavery

Sugar goes from east Med. → Atlantic islands → across places

The European presence and relative dominance on the African coast was due to their maritime power, which gave them effective control over deepwater sailing. But on the coast itself they were often dependent on local peoples. Anchored offshore while a few of their number negotiated on land, with local Africans in charge of the smaller boats navigating the often treacherous coastal waters, Europeans could never be fully at ease. Yet even after they realized that trade rather than warfare was the most lucrative as well as the most secure means of dealing with Africans, the slaving system remained permeated by violence. From their initial point of enslavement in Africa through to life on the plantations, the Africans endured a culture of violence at the mercy of their various owners. But on the coast and inland, with myriad local variations depending on geography as well as political and social systems, the negotiation of African slaves was simply that: a trade. The transformation of this trade from a small-scale local operation into a massive global enterprise was brought about by events on the other side of the Atlantic, and dictated above all by the rise of the sugar economy.

Sugar being made into loaves in the late Middle Ages.

Cane sugar had long been a luxury commodity in Europe, restricted by its cost to the upper reaches of society, who used it to sweeten other exotic imports such as coffee, tea and chocolate. Crusaders returning to northern Europe had brought back sugar from the Holy Land, and gradually the cultivation of sugar cane was developed in other suitable spots in the Mediterranean: Cyprus, Crete, North Africa and southern Spain. It was grown on plantations, but

OPPOSITE A Brazilian sugar mill, painted in the mid-17th century.

French representation of African distress at losing relatives to a Marseilles slave ship, 1764.

The harbour of Principe, in the Gulf of Guinea, 1727. The island was one of the last provisioning stops for many slave ships before heading across the Atlantic.

the workers used in sugar cultivation were generally free. As Europeans ventured into the Atlantic, beyond their traditional trading and sailing locations, they discovered new regions which could sustain sugar cultivation. Cane was planted in Madeira, the Canaries, the Cape Verde Islands and (unsuccessfully) in the Azores. Wherever the crop took root, it was cultivated on plantations which, from the first, needed plenty of manageable labour. They also required new supplies of workers to replace those who did not survive the heavy labouring regimes. When sugar was developed in the islands of Sao

A Prospect from Sea of ye Harbour of Princefs belonging to ye Portugueze.

The ISLAND of PRINCESS, lyes between the Islands of Ferdinando Po & St Thomé in the Latitude of 1 Degree 30 Minutes N. all belonging to ye Portugueze. This Island is very Woody, & breeds Abundance of Monkeys; insomuch, that it is not Safe to walk in the Woods without a Gun. The Harbour is very convenient to Carreen Ships in, and most Ships Bound from Africa to America with Slaves put in here for Wood, Water, &c.

Tome and Principe, in the Gulf of Guinea, it seemed both natural and logical for the Portuguese settlers to turn for labour to the African coast, only 400 km (250 miles) away. The islands flourished not only as staging posts for ships heading to Portugal but also, later, for vessels making for the Guinea current which helped to carry them westwards to the early settlements of the Americas. A link was clearly established: sugar production thrived when it was undertaken on plantations, and those plantations seemed best worked by imported African slaves.

In the Americas this process was more complex. Colonists tried a host of agricultural experiments, and various forms of labour – local Indians, indentured Europeans, free labour – often worked side by side. However, wherever the planters determined that sugar was the most appropriate local crop, they also decided that African slaves provided the best labour solution. Not only were large numbers of workers required to grow it, but the cane then needed to be turned into crude sugar. It was crushed, boiled and distilled in a rough industrial process which paralleled the arduous labour in the fields nearby. Indeed, the tell-tale signs of sugar plantations were the windmills and factory chimneys dotting the tropical landscape. Once refined, the sugar was packed into hogshead barrels and dispatched to the nearest quayside for the ships returning to Europe. There it was refined further and sold to a voracious market of sugar consumers.

The more land the colonists turned over to sugar cultivation, the more Africans they required. And the more sugar those slaves produced for export to Europe, the greater the demand for yet more

Drinking chocolate became acceptable and fashionable by the addition of cane sugar. These three tin-glazed earthenware chocolate cups, made in Lombardy about 1740–45, are painted with figures in Chinese and European dress. They were probably part of a set of eleven of various shapes and designs that belonged to Sir Hans Sloane (1660–1753), whose collection became the foundation of the British Museum.

Sugar hard to create as hard to grow

Moulin a sucre

Sucrerie

Canamelles

Simplistic late 17th-century French engraving of sugar cane being crushed and processed.

Coffee, tea and chocolate, represented by drinkers from Arabia, China and the Americas.

sugar from the expanding markets of European consumers. Africans and their local-born offspring were employed at every stage of the process: planting and cutting the cane, converting the cane into sugar in the factory, and transporting and shipping the hogsheads of sugar to the waiting ships. The plantations became remarkably varied and complex workplace societies based on the labour and skills of men and women, young and old.

From the growth of this apparently simple industry to produce sugar for the West emerged a quite extraordinary international economy and financial system. Africans were shipped across the Atlantic in ever-growing numbers to produce more and more cane sugar in order to satisfy the cravings of Europeans, who were becoming accustomed to food and especially drinks sweetened with sugar. Coffee, tea and chocolate, all exotic products from the far edges of the trading world, were made palatable to Western taste by the addition of cane sugar cultivated, processed and transported by Africans in the Americas. The system depended on a range of European industries to build and maintain the slave ships and to supply the plantations with imported hardware – tools, seeds and plants, foodstuffs, firearms – as well as imported labour. And everything hinged on outside finance for borrowing, lending and insuring, all to the great enhancement of first Europe's major cities and later new American centres of trade and finance.

The European expansion into the Americas is a well-known story, personified by the discoveries of Christopher Columbus on his early voyages seeking routes to the East. He was also empowered to secure islands en route, and at first the Caribbean islands seemed ideal for tropical cultivation. But their prospects were soon overshadowed by the treasures revealed in the subsequent discovery of the Aztec and Inca empires. Moreover, when sugar cultivation was first tried in both the Caribbean and Brazil, the usual labour problems quickly surfaced. The local Indians died out or simply drifted away from the strenuous demands. Both the Spaniards and Portuguese already had ample experience of using African slave labour at home and on their Atlantic islands, so faced with labour shortages in the Americas they again turned to African slaves. Settlers began to demand ever more Africans for their plantations, sometimes with the

Bartolomé de las Casas, a 16th-century Spanish bishop who defended indigenous peoples of the Americas against exploitation. He became known as 'the apostle of the Indians'.

The establishment of Christianity and the exchange of gifts: an imaginary encounter between Columbus and native peoples of the Caribbean.

Sugar Plantations

Brazilian sugar plantations (*engenhos*) were first established on the coast or riversides before the settlers moved inland. They were financed, organized and operated along the lines of previous plantations in the Mediterranean. Initially small, they produced low amounts of sugar (and income) and required relatively little capital investment. At first they relied on local Indian labour. But it soon became clear that Africans – even imported at a cost – were more productive. By the end of the 16th century, African slaves dominated the plantations, fuelling the demand for African imports. The plantations required the skills of artisans as well, but as they grew larger they needed ever more labourers, thereby becoming ever more African. They took on the form of modern factories: places of production based on a highly structured system. The sugar factory required a regular and uninterrupted flow of raw cane from the fields to satisfy its greedy machinery, so gangs of labourers, skilled and unskilled, were organized within a regime that wove the fieldwork tasks (cutting, stacking, loading) into the factory processes. From the plantations flowed not only a stream of highly prized sugar but the very nature of slavery itself.

Mid-17th-century view of Engenho Real, a Brazilian sugar factory. In the distance are ships preparing to transport the sugar abroad.

support of the Church, perhaps in the hope of sparing the local Indians. The drift to African slave labour in the Americas thus seems to follow a familiar pattern in which Europeans – led by Spain and Portugal – turned to labour systems they had already pioneered and proved viable in the eastern Atlantic.

African slaves had sailed to the Americas on Columbus's second voyage in 1493, and the Spanish Crown granted an *Asiento* to the Portuguese in 1513 authorizing them to transport African slaves to the Spanish colonies. However, the real growth in the early demand for slaves came not from the Spanish but from the Portuguese settlements in Brazil, where sugar cultivation began to expand first in Bahia and Pernambuco, especially after 1575. From small beginnings in a tiny part of this vast region, by the end of the century the

Brazilian sugar plantations had become completely dependent on imported African slaves. And by then, slaves were leaving Africa in huge numbers. By 1600, around 200,000 Africans had been shipped from West Africa as slaves to various destinations.

end of 1800s
all slaves in Brazil

Up to this point, the origins and development of African slavery in the Atlantic are broadly related to the story of Portuguese and Spanish maritime adventures and trade. But the Iberian system was too tempting to remain a monopoly. The rise of other European maritime powers ensured that they too would want a share of the lucrative business of slave trading and colonial settlement using African enslaved labour.

The English involvement in West Africa began, like that of the other European powers, with speculative voyages of trade and adventure. Inevitably English merchants trading to and from Iberia learned of the prospects available on the African coast. In 1555 (and again in 1556) William Towerson became the first Englishman to

A Brazilian sugar mill, illustrated in an atlas of 1710 showing Pernambuco, centre of the Brazilian sugar industry.

Sir John Hawkins, 1581, a successful Elizabethan sailor and adventurer as well as one of England's first slave traders.

embark on slave trading, followed a few years later by John Hawkins – this time with the support of Elizabeth I. Although the Queen had her own political reasons for becoming involved, she was also naturally keen to promote profitable trade and to make the most of any opportunities to expand her country's power, preferably at the expense of her European rivals. The English trade to and from Africa was on a very small scale, but along with other European powers, notably the Dutch and the French, they were acutely aware of the potential. But when the northern Europeans sought to enter the slave trade, they found that it was effectively controlled by the Portuguese and Spaniards, sanctioned by various *Asiento* treaties and secured by the Vatican through a papal bull which granted them each a monopoly in their own area of the Atlantic.

The Dutch were the first to make major inroads into this Iberian monopoly. In the late 16th century, the 'Golden Age' of the Dutch Republic, they temporarily seized control of Brazil and established

I have given permission...to Lorenzo de Gorrevod...to take to the Indies, the islands and the mainland...four thousand negro slaves both male and female, provided they be Christians...

Spanish royal slave trade license, 1518[1]

Surga

This map of Barbados in 1657, only a generation after the British seized it, shows the island being rapidly converted to sugar production.

their own outposts on the African slave coast. The Dutch also gave a major boost to English colonial aspirations in the Atlantic. The British used Dutch money, and Dutch expertise in sugar cultivation and manufacture, when they began to secure their own American colonies in the early 17th century. Settlers in St Kitts and Barbados greatly benefited from this Dutch investment when they began establishing their own sugar plantations. But, as settlers elsewhere discovered, sugar was not an immediate triumph.

Across the Americas, colonists tried a host of crops – cotton and tobacco, for example – before deciding that sugar was best suited to cultivation in the tropical colonies. And where sugar took hold, in the Caribbean, it quickly pushed aside other crops, though it never totally replaced them. In the process, plantations grew bigger and employed more and more Africans. Beginning in Brazil and moving through the West Indian islands, sugar came to dominate the landscape. Moreover, the plantations utterly transformed the landscape itself, changing the very look, the land patterns, even the flora and fauna of the sugar-growing regions. As it did so, sugar also transformed the local populations.

Native peoples were swept aside and moved away or simply died out. In their place, an increasingly African population evolved:

OPPOSITE View of Elmina at the time of Dutch control, late 17th or early 18th century.

legions of African slaves owned and worked by small bands of white settlers and a growing number of people of mixed race. Africans dominated the peopling of the Americas for three centuries, between the emergence of sugar in Brazil in the 1540s through to the 1820s. African men and women toiled side by side in the cane fields: though planters generally preferred young males, they used whoever was physically capable of doing the demanding work. Men tended to do the processing work in the sugar 'factories' (a word used in the sugar industry long before it was adopted in European industry).

By the 1820s more than 11 million people had crossed the Atlantic to settle in the Americas, but of these only 2.5 million were

If you go to Barbados you shal see a flourishing Iland...I believe they have bought this year no lesse than a thousand Negroes, and the more they buie, the better able they are to buye...

George Downing to John Winthrop, Governor of Connecticut, 1645[2]

Merchants, slaves and the military mingle in a busy Caribbean dockside scene at Christiansted, a Danish outpost on St Croix, 1798.

Europeans – the rest were African slaves. Of course, the Africans were not scattered evenly across the newly settled Americas but were concentrated in particular places, notably in Brazil and the Caribbean, primarily because of sugar. Already by 1650 some 800,000 Africans had been removed from West Africa in slave ships, and of that number perhaps a quarter had been transported to Brazil.

Cane transported by oxen to be crushed in a windmill on Antigua, supervised by a slave with a white man looking on, 1823.

Though the British were not the pioneers of the Atlantic slave trade, they proved themselves quick and willing learners, and within a century they had come to dominate the transatlantic transportation of enslaved Africans, supplying not only their own but also other nation's colonies. Again, it had small beginnings: the British sugar revolution was effectively pioneered in St Kitts and Barbados, but it was Oliver Cromwell's seizure of Jamaica from Spain in 1655 which transformed the story. Thereafter Jamaica absorbed vast numbers of Africans, with many others shipped onwards to Spanish settlements in Central America.

All the major European maritime powers became slave traders, or used African slave labour in their American colonies. Spain, Portugal, Holland, France, Britain, Denmark, Brandenburg (in Germany) – all found the potential profits of Atlantic slavery irresistible. The end result was that, within a century, what had started as a speculative European attempt to develop trade with West Africa had been utterly transformed. By 1700 African humanity – not African gold and spices – had become the most valuable of African exports,

takes 200 years or so

Meticulously surveyed and drafted plan of Lucky Valley Estate, 1769. It was owned by Edward Long, one of Jamaica's wealthiest planters, who was also a prominent politician and historian.

Oliver Cromwell planned to attack Spain's New World possessions in 1655 through an offensive referred to as 'The Western Design'. The main aim was to take the Caribbean island of Hispaniola (present-day Santo Domingo and Haiti) and use it as a base against Spain's trade and empire. With an army made up of men from Britain and others recruited in Barbados and the small English islands in the West Indies, the invasion of Hispaniola proved a disaster, so the survivors retreated to their ships and headed for the more weakly defended Spanish island of Jamaica. It was easily taken, and the British army was eventually disbanded and the soldiers became settlers on the land. Jamaica had basically served as a provisioning ground for the Spanish elsewhere, but the new British colonists were more persistent settlers, trying a range of agricultural crops before eventually turning to sugar. They first employed a combination of free, indentured and slave labour, as their predecessors had done in Barbados. But as sugar became the dominant crop, the African slave became the typical plantation worker. From such unlikely origins, a century later Jamaica had become the jewel in the British Caribbean crown.

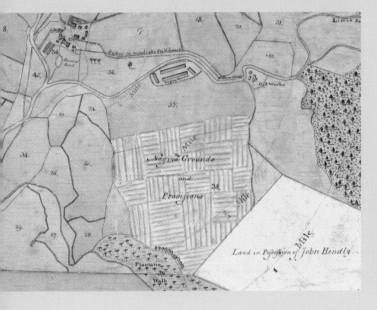

thanks to the economic importance of sugar and the tide of sugar development which swept across the tropical Americas.

What seems curious to modern eyes is that Europeans of all nations and social groups were so untroubled by moral or religious doubts about African slavery. Few complained that shiploads of Africans were bought and bartered for, shipped and traded, like any other commercial commodity. There were, it is true, periodic objections: moral and religious protests about the fundamental ethical issues involved. More common, however, were protests about the need to ameliorate the treatment of Africans, if only to secure a safer

Atlantic crossing or to ensure a better price at the slave auctions. But such voices were few and easily drowned by the clatter of profitable business. Defenders of the slave trade had only to point to the forests of masts in all the major slaving ports – Nantes, Bordeaux, Bristol, Liverpool or Glasgow – to silence their critics. What were the complaints of a few people of sensibility compared to the undoubted bounty flowing from the slave ships?

people don't see a problem at all

The sugar-growing regions of the tropical Americas became a new image of Africa. With only a few local exceptions, Africans and their descendants far outnumbered whites in the sugar colonies. On the plantations, Africans greatly outnumbered their owners and managers. But other changes were also at work. In all slave colonies new strata of society emerged: people who were the offspring of Africans and Europeans. Such groups made the social structure of local life more complex and served to confuse the harsh divide forged by slavery between black and white.

This African numerical preponderance is part of a complex historical question. How was it, both on the slave ships and on the sugar plantations, that such small minorities of white people managed to control and dominate such overwhelming numbers of subject people? Stated crudely, how did the Atlantic slave system, with its huge African majority and its small slave-owning minority, stay in place for so long? Why did the slaves not simply throw off their shackles? That question was nowhere more striking than on the Atlantic slave ships.

ships put Africans down

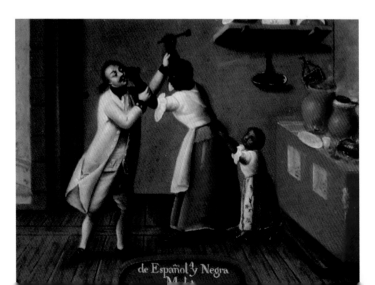

An 18th-century Mexican domestic scene illustrating the 'mixing of races'.

de Español y Negra

Chapter 3

sickness/disease
crammed
threatened
so re mutiny
looked at
like animals
kill the
rebellious
harsh daily
life in general
degrading
treatment

punished strictly cruelly
bad weather
kept from any possible
weapon
sick people are something
left for dead or mistreated
over-cruelty to prove
a point
plantation trans. is
more sea (PTIS)

The Middle Passage

At its height it was hard to deny the massive benefits of the Atlantic slave trade to the merchants and industries of Europe, and making it all possible were the slave ships ferrying Africans west across the Atlantic in what came to be called the Middle Passage. There may have been as many as 40,000 slave voyages (we have details of 35,000), and although the very great majority of Africans on the ships survived to land in the Americas, a large number arrived in a wretched condition. Many died in the immediate aftermath, succumbing to sickness and diseases that resulted from enslavement and conditions on the ships. Yet the aim of the slave ships was not to kill or cripple their cargo, but to deliver strong, healthy Africans to the markets in the Americas. Even so, perhaps the most enduring popular perception of slavery is the level of death, illness and suffering on the ships. And if there is one graphic image that remains familiar to this day, it is surely the plan of the slave ship *Brookes* (1788), a Liverpool vessel of 297 tons which carried 609 Africans in the last years of the slave trade.

In the early days of British slave trading, the Crown awarded a monopoly to the Royal African Company, but it was unable to satisfy the plantation colonies' voracious appetite for imported Africans. After 1713 the trade was thrown open and thereafter the growth in slave trading was extraordinary, as merchants in a string of ports rushed to join the trade in African humanity. They often joined together in syndicates to finance and insure the ships and their cargoes through a complex European commercial network in which

OPPOSITE One in ten slave ships experienced some form of African revolt. This illustration captures the mayhem and desperate violence involved.

An image of prosperous respectability: Charles Goore (1701–83), merchant, slave trader and twice mayor of Liverpool.

Chocolate was made palatable to Western taste by the addition of sugar. This chocolate party (*chocolatada*) is illustrated on a Valencian tile panel of the early 18th century.

all parties hoped to benefit from the ensuing profits. They filled the outbound ships heading to Africa with goods from across Europe's industries (metal goods from Birmingham and Sheffield, textiles from Lancashire, equipment, firearms and luxury goods such as French wines and brandies). From small beginnings, the Atlantic slave trade grew to generate an immense web of commercial and industrial activity, bringing material wealth and well-being to its major players, and transforming the tastes of Western Europe through slave-grown tropical produce. The trade also transformed some of Europe's major ports, most notably Liverpool and Bordeaux.

The British tended to trade along the coastline from Sene-Gambia to the Congo, but especially from West and Central Africa. By the end of the trade in 1807, the British had shipped about 3.5 million Africans across the Atlantic, and one African in five had crossed the Atlantic in a Liverpool ship. The city's shipbuilders could hardly keep pace with the demand for new vessels. In the last twenty years of the legal trade, shipbuilders in Liverpool constructed 469 slave ships.

He commanded Vessels...from nearly 200 to 300 tons. The Number of Slaves...was from 500 to 600...The Slave Ships at Liverpool are built on Purpose for this Trade...

James Penny, slave captain, evidence to the British Parliament, 1789[1]

Only ten years before the abolition of the trade, in 1797, the Liverpool slave ship *Watt* was built in Liverpool for local slave trade merchants Watt and Walker.

Slave ships came in all shapes and sizes. We know of one weighing a mere 11 tons, while the largest was almost 600 tons. The ships changed as the trade developed. Many were custom-built, and by the late 18th century many vessels were constructed in North America (notably Newport, Rhode Island). But large numbers were normal merchant ships, adapted for the special purpose of carrying human cargoes. In time, the men who owned and ran them perfected the system of loading the maximum number of Africans into a confined space, sailing across the Atlantic efficiently and speedily, and delivering huge numbers of people to their destination. In fact the crossings got faster, largely because of improved ship design and navigational

LEFT The heart of Bristol's slave trade: the docks and quay (also known as Broad Quay) in 1760.

FOLLOWING PAGES Drawn by a Royal Navy officer: the 'illicit' Portuguese slave ship *Diligenté*, with 600 Africans on board, was captured by HMS *Pearl* and taken to Nassau in 1838.

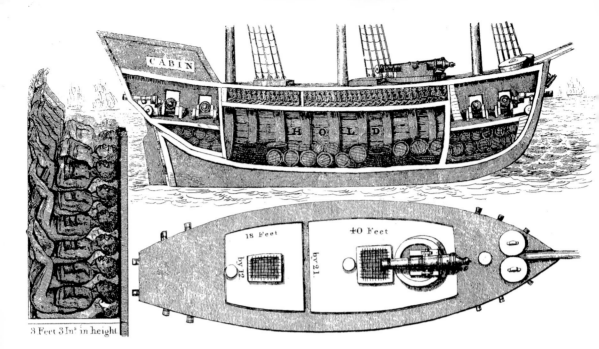

CABIN

H O L D

18 Feet

by 12

40 Feet

by 21

3 Feet 3 In⁵ in height

A popular 19th-century image of a slave ship, illustrating overcrowding of Africans in every available space.

practices. Quite simply, the slave traders got better at what they did.

Ships sailed from all corners of the Atlantic world, though the trade came to be dominated by the major maritime powers and their main ports: London, Bristol and Liverpool, Nantes and Bordeaux, Newport (Rhode Island) and Rio de Janeiro. But even tiny ports sought their share of the increasingly lucrative trade. Who today would think of St Malo, Chester or Lyme Regis as ports that dispatched ships to the slave coast?

When such ships arrived on the African coast, the carpenters rigged up extra shelving below decks and constructed safety barriers and defences above – with guns pointed towards the decks to ensure the crew's safety in any confrontation with their unwilling human cargo. Slave ships were rarely able to fill up quickly with Africans after arriving on the coast. Instead, they lingered for months, trading and bartering for batches of Africans. Sometimes small craft ferried cap-

[The Africans] are brought out into a large plain, where the surgeons examine every part of every one of them, to the smallest member, men and women being all stark naked.

Jean Barbot, French slaver, 1682[2]

tives to the ships at anchor, or sailors might go ashore to negotiate with Africans traders and middlemen. The people they purchased had often been enslaved many months earlier and many miles into the interior, about which Europeans still knew very little. The enslaved Africans now saw Europeans for the first time and found themselves examined like livestock by the ships' captains and surgeons, who were looking for frailties and defects – all with an eye to profitable sale in the Americas.

The Africans then had to survive for months on board the slave ship before it even began the difficult Atlantic crossing. As the numbers of Africans on board increased, the officers and crew were soon greatly outnumbered. But the slavers developed well-tried routines and practices to keep their African prisoners secure, reasonably healthy, and occupied. At all times the sailors were conscious that the Africans posed an acute danger both to the crew and to the ship. Although some slaves, especially the women and children, might be allowed certain freedoms on deck while the ships were anchored offshore, gangs of males – healthy young men, extremely angry about what had happened to them – posed a constant danger. The slave ship was basically a floating prison, and the Africans were controlled by a disciplinary regime that became increasingly draconian as their numbers mounted. According to slave captain John Atkins in 1735:

A rebellious African, in chains, on the deck of a slave ship, 1801.

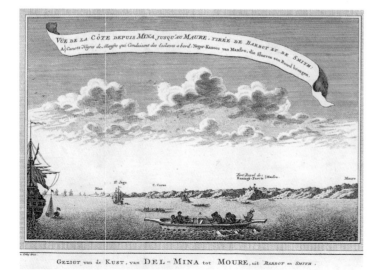

View of African slave forts including Elmina: in the foreground, Africans are rowed from shore to waiting slave ships.

'The success of a voyage depends first on well sorting and well timing of a cargo, secondly, in a knowledge of the places of trade, thirdly, in dramming well with English spirits, and fourthly, in timely furnishing proper food for the slaves, fifthly, in dispatch, and lastly, the good order and management of slaves when on board.'[3]

Discipline on board the slave ships could only function effectively through the use of the metal goods that became the mainstay of slave ship life. Europe's iron industries disgorged vast quantities of chains, fetters, manacles and restraints specifically manufactured for this purpose. Today, images of the chains of slavery are seen as evoking African subjection. But the opposite is also true: they are evidence of African rebellion. Throughout the history of the slave trade, it was these physical restraints which enabled sailors to ship huge numbers of Africans to the Americas. Without the manacles and chains, the crews would surely have been overwhelmed, so it is worth thinking of chains also as a symbol of African defiance.

As the slave ships lingered on the coast, and as conditions on board deteriorated through the sheer pressure of numbers, the risks of African violence increased. It was at this stage, still within sight of Africa, that most slave insurrections erupted. Once the ship ventured into the Atlantic, the terrors of the ocean voyage only compounded the Africans' physical distress. Chained below deck in cramped conditions for much of the time, occasionally taken up and exercised on deck in small groups, their life on board would become even more unbearable in the turmoil of bad weather. In a storm the crew were hard-pressed simply to sail the ship and were forced to ignore the needs of the Africans, whose ordeal was now at its worst. Disease spread easily in the filth of communal incarceration. The Africans – numbered, rarely named, in the ship logs – succumbed to a variety of diseases, but especially dysentery ('the bloody flux'). Corpses were simply thrown overboard as the ship struggled westwards. Not surprisingly, the slave ships stank: their notorious stench could be detected miles downwind.

ABOVE AND BELOW
Metal neck restraints, basic tools of the late 18th-century slave trade.

A Slave Voyage

On 11 August 1750 the *Duke of Argyle*, a 140-ton ship with a crew of 30 men and captained by John Newton, departed Liverpool for West Africa. Newton faced persistent disciplinary trouble with his crew (he had to hand one over to the tender mercies of the Royal Navy). The ship spent seven months plying up and down the African coast south of Sierra Leone, slowly filling with Africans, who were traded for the various goods imported from Liverpool. Africans began to die as soon as they were brought on board – mainly of 'the bloody flux' (dysentery). When the ship turned to cross the Atlantic on 22 May 1751, Newton had 161 Africans on board. By the time he docked at St Johns in Antigua on 3 July 1751, after 43 days at sea, 25 Africans had died. The ship stayed in Antigua a little over a month before heading back to sea on 13 August. It was a long haul back, and the ship was battered by several Atlantic storms. But on 7 October the *Duke of Argyle* arrived back in Liverpool after an absence of 14 months. In addition to his wages, John Newton received a handsome dividend of £257. By that time, the surviving Africans had doubtless been sold and scattered to plantations across Antigua.

John Newton (1725–1807), once a slave ship captain, became a famous cleric and ardent abolitionist.

The ABOLITION of the SLAVE TRADE.
Or the Inhumanity of Dealers in human flesh exemplified in Capt.ⁿ Kimber's treatment of a young Negro Girl of 15 for her Virgin Modesty

Isaac Cruikshank's famous caricature, 'The Abolition of the Slave Trade' (1792), depicting Capt. Kimber's notorious torture of a 15-year-old African girl.

The length of time spent at sea varied greatly, the duration of the voyage determined partly by the point of departure and the destination. Currents and prevailing winds could deliver slave ships from Angola relatively quickly to northeast Brazil; similarly, ships from the Guinea coast could make landfall in Barbados in six weeks. But bad weather and mishaps with food and water (to say nothing of conflict) often prolonged a voyage, and the Africans paid a heavy price for extended periods at sea. Some simply gave up: slave ships had netting rigged around the vessel to prevent African suicides.

Through all this the crew, while trying to sail the vessel, and often reduced in numbers by the heavy death toll on the African coast, faced ranks of sick, terrified and angry Africans. Working on a slave ship was the most unpleasant of all deepwater sailing duties. Only the roughest and most desperate men signed up, perhaps when drunk or to pay off debts, sometimes out of ignorance of the conditions. However, despite the dangers, during the century before abolition in 1807 about a third of a million sailors worked on British slave ships: it was a massive industry. From the beginning the crew were wary of the Africans, and their wariness quickly turned to fear. In a careless moment, a tool – or any piece of wood or metal – left unattended could become a lethal weapon in African hands, perhaps

Slave Ship Surgeons

Doctors on slave ships were not always qualified, but after 1789 British slavers were obliged to carry one. Their first job was to examine Africans before purchase, advising captains about the ailments and problems to look for, and then to prepare Africans for sale in the Americas. On the long Atlantic crossing they might attempt to maintain some semblance of health and hygiene among the Africans shackled below decks. But

often there was little they could do in the face of contagious diseases and filthy conditions. The papers, journals and publications of slave surgeons present a miserable litany of African death and suffering. Christopher Bowes, for example, was surgeon on the *Lord Stanley* in 1792. In June he recorded the medical details – and the deaths – of the Africans on board in the following manner:

The man slave No. 8 not much pain. The man No. 4 the same as yesterday. The man No. 5 rather worse. A girl No. 4 complained of a pain in the head...at 3 a.m. she was seized with delirium, a few hours after convulsions came on and at 8 a.m. she died.[4]

It was the evidence of such men, presented to the public and the British Parliament after 1788, that provided powerful, irrefutable evidence of the human suffering at the heart of the slave trade: it was evidence which won over legions of support for abolition.

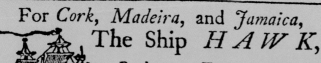

For *Cork, Madeira,* and *Jamaica,*
The Ship *H A W K,*
Burthen 400 Tons, 24 Guns, and Men anſwerable ;
JOHN SYERS, *Commander.*
For Freight or Paſſage, apply to the Maſter, or to Mr. Joſeph Maneſty.
.*.* She will ſail on, or before, the Firſt of next Month.
N. B. Surgeons and Surgeons Mates, are wanted, for Ships in the African and American Trade.——Apply to the Printer.

Advertisement to recruit surgeons, who were vital for a successful slave voyage.

OPPOSITE The *Brookes* slave ship, published by the Quaker publisher James Phillips, 1789. It became the most durable image of the slave trade, used by abolitionists everywhere.

plunging the crew into a desperate fight for survival against insurgent Africans. Slave ships were armed with strategically placed guns pointing inwards towards the decks, where rebellious Africans might emerge from their prisons below.

The slave ships became a floating hell. Even by contemporary standards, the level of violence needed to maintain control was exceptional. The reprisals against defeated African rebels on slave ships were deliberately extreme: public shootings, dismemberment and beheading generally followed failed shipboard rebellions. Savage punishments were inflicted both to punish the rebels and intimidate the survivors. The French slave trader Jean Barbot urged severity: 'Spare no effort to repress their insolence and, as an example to the others, sacrifice the lives of all the most mutinous. This will terrify the others and keep them obedient.'[5] Africans quickly learned what would happen to them if they rebelled and failed. And even if they managed to overwhelm the crew, how could they return home or even sail the ship?

Drawing of Africans below decks on an 'illicit' slave ship seized by the Royal Navy, 1846.

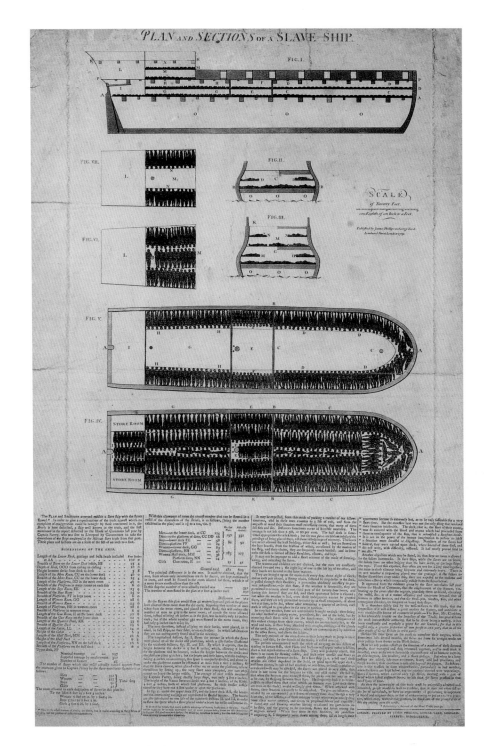

PLAN AND SECTIONS OF A SLAVE-SHIP.

A variety of metal restraints used to control and torture slaves – mask and collar, leg shackles and spurs – in a woodcut from *The Penitential Tyrant*, published in New York in 1807.

Of course, once the ships headed into the Atlantic the Africans had no idea where they were, where they were going or what was planned for them, aside from shipboard rumours and gossip. Many initially believed they would be eaten, but then learned from sailors and Africans working on and around the ships that they were going across the sea to work. Yet it was hard to make sense of this as the vessel sailed on for many weeks with nothing in sight (when they were allowed on deck) except the Atlantic in all its vastness. They were surrounded by turbulent ocean and the distant horizon on all sides. The miseries of bad weather, the slow erosion of illness and occasional deaths, combined with the harshness of the daily regime, produced a hellish life for all the Africans. Their ailments were often contagious and spread quickly in the diseased squalor of the slave decks, regardless of any efforts of the crew and the ship surgeon to maintain some sort of order and cleanliness below decks.

This was the experience common to all Africans on the Atlantic slave ships. Though there was plenty of individual violence, the basic miseries were not a result of capricious brutality from the crew. What afflicted every single African was the regime of the slave ship. Carrying huge numbers of enslaved people in a crowded ship, manned by a small band of sailors, necessitated a tight and unflinchingly brutal routine. Cruelty versus kindness was not the issue. It was the ship itself, the way it was planned, designed and managed, which inflicted the most suffering on the Africans. Though the graphic image of a slave ship with Africans packed head to toe, sardine-like, was a caricature, it captured the squalid intimacy of life between decks as described by Alexander Falconbridge, a former slave surgeon, in 1788:

> They are frequently stowed too close, as to admit of no other posture than lying on their sides. Neither will the height between decks, unless directly under the gratings, permit them the indulgence of an erect posture.[6]

Chained in close proximity to each other (though women and children tended to be allowed greater freedom), eating communally in filthy conditions, struggling to get to the 'necessary tubs' to relieve themselves, Africans found themselves in a nightmare world of filth, suffering and dying. It is true that some slave ships had few casualties (and the death rates tended to decline over time), but most Africans endured unspeakably horrible and dangerous conditions through-out the Atlantic crossing. They were handled roughly, often in the most intimate and degrading ways, by sailors who were terrified of them. The two sides, black and white (though black crewmen were to be found on the slave ships), glared at each other with hate and fear throughout the voyage, and the situation would get even worse if supplies ran low. Sometimes this resulted from bad planning, or if a voyage was prolonged by bad weather. Other times, barrels of water and food rotted, often attacked by rodents and termites. With sup-plies low, everyone was put on rations and the crew anxiously scanned the horizon for land. When it finally appeared, the Africans entered the next miserable phase of their captivity.

In the days before landing the crew prepared the Africans for sale. Now was the time to disguise, as far as possible, the Africans' ship-board ailments. They were washed and scrubbed, their skin given a healthy sheen by the application of palm oil. The awaiting purchasers, however, would know how to spot the tell-tale signs of sickness or injury. Some slaves were beyond disguise or recovery. The most

This image of Africans, neatly organized below decks on a slave ship in the 1830s, captures the overcrowding but misses the chaotic squalor.

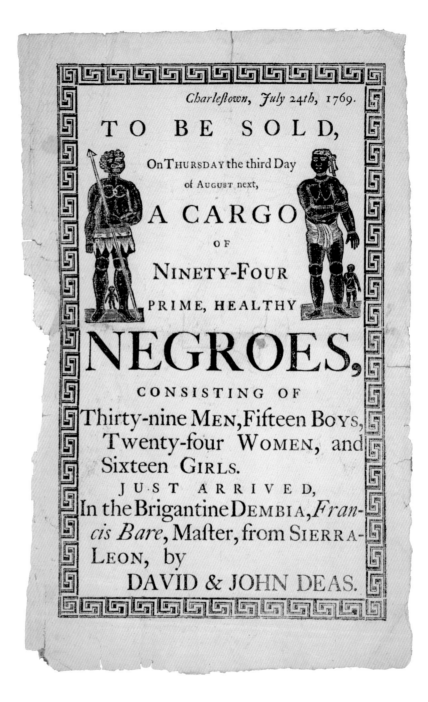

Charlestown, July 24th, 1769.

TO BE SOLD,

On THURSDAY the third Day of AUGUST next,

A CARGO

OF

NINETY-FOUR

PRIME, HEALTHY

NEGROES,

CONSISTING OF

Thirty-nine MEN, Fifteen BOYS, Twenty-four WOMEN, and Sixteen GIRLS.

JUST ARRIVED,

In the Brigantine DEMBIA, *Francis Bare*, Master, from SIERRA-LEON, by

DAVID & JOHN DEAS.

Broadside advertisement from Charleston, 1769, offering a cargo of 94 Africans for sale.

wretched and grievously sick were the infamously named 'refuse slaves' – those apparently on the verge of death or too weakened to work, who were bought up cheaply as a job-lot and taken away to be fed and tended in the hope that some might survive and recover, and thereby provide a profit for the speculator who had bought them.

On arrival Africans were sold in a variety of ways. Some were delivered to merchants who had previously placed an order. Others were sent to auctions, which were often advertised in advance with information about the slaves' origins, condition and prices. Worst perhaps were the 'scrambles', when terrifying stampedes of eager purchasers would rush among the Africans at a given signal, grabbing the individuals they intended to buy. Those who were sold found themselves handed over to new owners, often travelling further great distances inland or even by sea before reaching their final destination on the plantations of the West Indies, Central or South America.

Not surprisingly after such strenuous travels, many did not long survive their early months in the Americas. But those who did now faced a lifetime's bondage, at work they had never before experienced, managed by people they did not understand but whose language they must quickly learn, even if only after a fashion. Most of the new arrivals were settled on plantations, though in time large numbers were to move into other kinds of work, whether on the new American frontiers, in transport, as domestic servants, or in urban or portside communities. Even plantation work varied hugely, depending on the nature of the crop, ranging from tobacco, coffee, rice or cotton to sugar. Sugar was notoriously the toughest – hence the never-ending need for fresh African labour for the sugar plantations.

But for all the variations in the work undertaken by slaves, for all the diversity among the Africans themselves with their varied languages, cultures and customs, and despite the different labour regimes which developed in the Americas, one group of slaves – 'shipmates' – were bound together by the single rudimentary fact that they had endured and survived the Atlantic crossing together, an experience that outsiders could barely comprehend.

The slave ships were a highly traumatic experience, which to this day remains difficult to recapture in words. Yet this was not simply because of capricious individual cruelty (though there was plenty of that), but because it was a system which could only function through violence, often on an epic scale. The slave voyages were based on a culture of cruelty that corrupted the men who worked the ships as much as it hurt its African victims. From the beginning, slave merchants, captains and doctors debated the best means of carrying so many Africans successfully across the Atlantic. Some advocated a more benign regime – treating and feeding the Africans better, for example – so as to land more healthy Africans in the Americas. But there were obvious limits to that policy, not least because the Africans were unwilling passengers. They did not want to be there and could only be kept on the ships by force. Sailors who disliked the job of

Slaves working in a Brazilian tobacco factory, 1792.

Une vente d'esclaves, à Rio-de-Janeiro.

commanding or corralling Africans across the Atlantic simply quit the slave ships for other work. The Atlantic slave trade created a circular problem, and there seemed no other way of providing the American plantations with what they wanted: regular supplies of new African labour. For all the cruelty, despite the inescapable deaths and suffering, and notwithstanding the abominations of daily life on the slave decks, the slave ships succeeded in delivering millions of African slaves to the Americas. For the Africans, with the traumas of the ships behind them, arrival meant the beginning of another nightmare – a lifetime's bondage and back-breaking work.

Grotesque public examination of a slave woman by a fat interested bidder at a public auction of slaves, alongside other worldly goods, in Rio de Janeiro.

Chapter 4

Destinations and Slave Life

What began as a haphazard dribble of Africans to the Americas soon became a steady flow of people to specific regions. Portuguese Brazil led the way. Europeans first established plantations on the coast and then inland. By the 18th century, Brazil was absorbing 20,000 Africans a year. Over the next century, a million Africans crossed the Atlantic to Brazil. And from sugar, slavery spilled into all corners of the Brazilian economy, from mining to cattle ranching.

The British followed a similar pattern, demanding ever more Africans for their Caribbean possessions, especially after the islands were turned over to sugar cultivation. At first, English activity in the region took the form of privateering, in the era when legendary pirates picked off Spanish treasure fleets heading home from the 'Spanish Main' through the Caribbean. This soon gave way to settlement and trade, and by the end of the 17th century sugar plantations were demanding increasing numbers of African slaves to cut back the untamed wilderness and bring it into profitable cultivation. As the global power of Spain and Portugal, and later of the Dutch, waned, Britain established military and commercial ascendancy. But Britain, in turn, was challenged by her arch-rival France, also keen to acquire Caribbean islands and convert them to tropical cultivation.

Europeans had no doubt that this link was critical: power and prosperity in the Atlantic flowed from American possessions, and in particular from slave cultivation in the tropics. By 1700 Barbados was home to 50,000 slaves, and the booming port of Bridgetown was the most prosperous town in British America. By then, something like a

OPPOSITE Slaves working in a Brazilian diamond mine, supervised by white men carrying whips, in a late 18th-century watercolour.

quarter of a million Africans had been settled in the British islands. It was Jamaica, however, that eventually became Britain's most valuable slave colony. By the mid-18th century the island had a slave population of some 118,000. The French islands followed a similar pattern.

Humbly represent that the trade of Africa is so necessary to England that the very being of the Plantations depends upon the negro servants for their works. Letter from an English merchant, 1663[1]

St Kitts, Guadaloupe, Martinique and, later and above all, St Domingue (Haiti) on Hispaniola became home to huge numbers of Africans. As early as 1700, in the region of 140,000 Africans had been settled in the French Caribbean islands. But at the same time, more than half a million Africans had been landed in Brazil, and perhaps 450,000 in the non-Spanish Caribbean. The slaves were flung, like battalions of soldiers, at the fertile but untamed wilderness

Recreation among the slaves: Africans play a game of cudgels in Dominica, c. 1779.

of the islands, toiling to bring the land into profitable cultivation.

The number of Africans transported to North America was smaller. They began arriving in 1619 but the flow did not accelerate until the development of tobacco plantations in Virginia and Maryland. By 1750 there were 145,000 slaves working there, while another 40,000 Africans had been shipped to the rice-growing areas of South Carolina. Only a small proportion of all Africans shipped across the Atlantic were sent to North America – perhaps only 5 per cent of the total. The reason is straightforward: the North American slave population was very fertile and grew rapidly. By the end of the 18th century, when the United States of America was founded, the new nation was already home to about 700,000 slaves. (Brazil at this stage had a million slaves.) Thereafter, as cotton boomed in the 'Deep South', the plantations there could be supplied with new slaves direct from the slave regions of the 'Old South' (Virginia, Maryland and South Carolina) and so had no need of the transatlantic slave trade.

Wherever sugar was the dominant crop, slave populations rarely saw natural increase. They expanded only by importing new con-

Potential purchasers inspecting and scrutinizing slaves at an auction in Charleston, South Carolina, 1856.

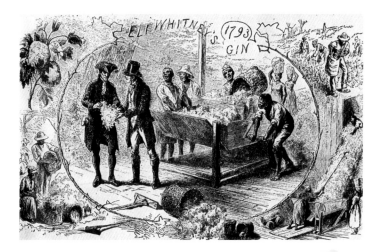

Eli Whitney's cotton gin, 1793, revolutionized the processing of cotton and made possible the expansion of the slave-based cotton industry of the Deep South.

signments of Africans in the slave ships. And the more the planters imported, the more they required for the arduous work on the sugar plantations. This persistent labour shortage was linked to the sexual ratio, reproduction rate and reduced life expectancy on the sugar plantations, as well as the damaging effects of the particularly harsh work in the hostile environment of sugar cultivation. Life as a sugar slave was, generally, tougher than most other forms of slave plantation labour in the Americas.

Not only did the Africans shipped to the Americas transform the face of the American colonies, they also cultivated crops which

The Negroes are encreased by fresh Supplies from Africa and the West India Islands, but also are very prolifick themselves; and they that are born there talk good English, and affect our Language, Habits and Customs.   Rev. Hugh Jones, writing about the Virginia colony, 1724[2]

OPPOSITE The cultivation and harvesting of indigo, a staple used in dyeing cloth.

changed the tastes and habits first of Europe and later the world at large. Tobacco (and snuff) from Virginia and Maryland, rice, indigo and naval stores from South Carolina, sugar, rum and coffee from the Caribbean – all and more were produced by African slave labour. Even the mahogany used in the finest of 18th-century furniture was logged by African slaves in Jamaica and Central America.

In the early days of colonial settlement, slave and free, black and

Pl. 1.

Fig. 1.

Fig. 2.

Fig. 3.

Fig. 17.

Fig. 7.

Fig. 8.

Fig. 9.

Fig. 5.

Fig. 11.

Fig. 13.

Fig. 14.

Fig. 16.

Fig. 12.

Fig. 4.

Fig. 12.

Benard direx.

Indigoterie, Travail du terrein pour planter l'Indigo et pour le recolter. 35

white (and sometimes local Indians) worked side by side. But that faded with the rise of the large plantations. The predominant form of slave labour was on a plantation, where the work was highly regimented and disciplined. Africans and their descendants were marshalled into gangs, the younger and stronger slaves undertaking the more severe, punitive forms of field work (planting, harvesting) while older, less robust groups performed less physically demanding tasks. In time, the plantations became much more than a place of labour: they became discrete communities, societies in which people lived out their entire lives. They were at once a workplace and an organic community which contained 'African villages' for the slave labour force and more elaborate – sometimes even grand – dwellings to house the small numbers of owners and managers. They contained factories (often very basic) where the cane was converted into sugar, and areas of land set aside for food cultivation. There were plots and gardens for the slaves, pens for animals and workshops for the manufacture and maintenance of plantation equipment. A variety of skilled people were responsible for specialized tasks, all of which added up to an increasingly complex plantation society.

Major and sometimes complex hierarchies and distinctions developed even among the ranks of the labouring slaves. For example,

A boiling house for sugar, a model of up-to-date machinery and layout, in Cuba, 1857.

Slave Work

Slave work varied enormously, mainly depending on the crop. Sugar made the harshest of demands: six months of heavy harvesting and gathering in hot tropical weather. Equally unpleasant was cultivating rice, which required labour in swampy conditions in snake-infested waters. Tobacco lacked the environmental dangers of sugar and rice, but though it was organized by task rather than gang labour, it had its own ceaseless and gruelling regime. And everywhere – whatever the work – slaves were subject to the whims and fads of owners and even passing strangers. Slavery was also never-ending: a life shaped and defined by labour, from the earliest years to the infirmities of old age. At first plantations were small: free and slave, black and white worked side by side at simple but onerous tasks of converting the land to profitable agriculture. But as the major crops began to dominate, plantations grew bigger, especially in sugar. The largest were complete communities, with housing sharply demarcated between slaves (in their village) and whites in homes at an appropriate distance away. Processing the harvested crops involved additional, often separate groups of workers. Each crop had to be carefully prepared and packed – in barrels, hogsheads, sacks or bales – for transport off the plantation and often for export across the Atlantic. The plantation was a highly organized system of labour. And it generated a wider – indeed global – tightly organized economy: ships arrived at certain times of the year to deliver Africans or to export the crops; finance, credit and imported goods were all carefully planned and ordered to meet specific needs and deadlines. It was, from first to last, a very modern form of industry, production and consumption.

Industrialized sugar cultivation – factory chimneys and steam train – with slave labour, Cuba, 1857.

American slaves bring a
week's cotton pickings
back from the fields.

there were marked differences between recently arrived Africans and local-born, between skilled and labouring slaves, between domestic and transport slaves. Against all the odds, some slaves even managed to improve themselves, using their skills and personal attributes to make a little money and enhance their lives. A Jamaican runaway in 1790 was described as speaking 'the English, French, Dutch, Danish and Portuguese languages'.[3] And an account of the variety of skilled slaves owned by George Mason in Virginia, one of the founders of the new United States, was given by his son: 'My father had among his slaves carpenters, coopers, sawyers, blacksmiths, tanners, curriers, shoemakers, spinners, weavers and knitters, and even a distiller.'[4]

Slaves were expected to work for their owners throughout their entire lives, from the early days of childhood through to old age or infirmity and the waning of their strength or abilities. But even in old age, tasks were found for slaves: looking after children, keeping watch or guarding animals. They were economic assets to be used to the maximum advantage of their owner.

The nature and rhythm of local work on plantations was dictated by the pattern and pace of the agricultural year. On sugar plantations, six months of the year were consumed by the heavy-duty tasks of cutting, gathering and processing the cane. In North America, rice cultivation in oppressive heat and swampy conditions was most similar to the sugar slavery of the Caribbean and Brazil. But unlike sugar, the work on rice plantations was organized not through gang labour but on a task system. With task work, slaves could set the

Family life on a 19th-century Brazilian plantation in the company of slaves and their children, with Christian artefacts on the wall.

All the horrors of slavery summed up in one illustration: an abolitionist caricature for a children's book of 1826.

pace of their own work and were not always troubled by the intrusive and often brutal demands of the slave gang leaders. On the tobacco plantations of the 'Upper South' in Virginia and Maryland, where free and enslaved labour often worked closely together, the crop took longer to come to fruition, and there too slaves worked not in gangs but at specific tasks. After 1800, cotton cultivation spread across a vast stretch of the American South. By 1860 the United States was producing 5 million bales of cotton each year. By then 4 million slaves lived in the USA, 60 per cent of whom worked in cotton, and 400,000 Americans owned slaves, most only a small number. But labour in the cotton fields, for all its hardships and indignities, tended not to be as oppressive or brutal as work in the sugar fields.

Of course, on all plantations, just as on the slave ships, every slave was at the mercy of the unpredictable whims of owners and overseers. Whatever physical hardships the particular crop might impose on a slave, these were often compounded by the threat of violence and sexual aggression. The lash was rarely far away and could be administered for the most inconsequential of reasons, or for sadistic fun. Women of all ages were exposed to sexual predators, whether slave owners, white employees or even passing visitors.

No. 4

THE PARTING "Buy us too".

FOR SALE

A likely young NEGRO

No. 3

THE SALE.

Slaves everywhere faced the possibility (and often the reality) of having their family and community lives shattered by upheaval and removal. They were property, simply chattels listed among their owners' possessions. When the owner died or fell on hard times, or when he or she divided up their possessions by will or as a gift, perhaps to a son or daughter who was marrying, then individual slaves found themselves scattered. Children were taken from parents and spouses removed. Some slave holders realized that such family break-ups had disastrous effects among their labour force and tried to avoid them. But as slavery expanded and demand for labour increased, slaves were inevitably shifted around regardless of their feelings to wherever their owners could demand a good price. In North America this was an especially grievous memory.

Abolitionist portrayals of the break-up of a slave family in America, c. 1863.

Women violated in this way had no chance of redress. Like the beatings and whippings, sexual assault was a common feature of slave life.

Along with these inescapable dangers, slaves faced insecurity and uncertainty. They could be (and often were) shifted and sold without warning, moved from one property to another, and sometimes removed great distances. Often they were relocated, at a stroke, from loved ones. Partners were divided, families split up, children removed, lovers disappeared. Slaves were simply counted among their owners' assets, to be sold, bartered, bequeathed and relocated as required by the quirks of economic circumstance. Whatever fragile family life they might manage to create could be damaged or destroyed by such upheavals, over which the individual slave had no control. Time and again, millions of people found themselves helpless in the face of a system which viewed the slave as a piece of property. When William Fitzhugh died in Virginia in 1703 he left nine slave families, four of whom lost children in the subsequent reorganization of their owner's property. In 1774, Thomas Thorpe died in the same colony, leaving 19 slaves who were then divided up among all of Thorpe's nine heirs.

Another abolitionist appeal to the heart: a slave owner orders the whipping of a pregnant slave, 1828.

Slavery and international trade: tobacco being sold at the quayside and loaded for export from North America, 1775.

Slaves were an economic asset and their owners sought to use them in the most profitable fashion. Their importance to their owners – slave traders and planters – was reflected in the monetary value those owners noted in their ship's logs and plantation ledgers, often entering the commercial value of the individual slave alongside his or her name, age, occupation and physical condition. Here were people, counted in their millions, whose lives were measured out by their monetary value to someone else. Africans carried an initial price on their heads when they first entered the slave ship and a new price when they were sold on landing in the Americas. Then, year after year, their value to their current owner in the Americas would rise and fall with fluctuations in their age, sickness or skills. In 1756 Thomas Thistlewood in Jamaica paid £43 for a 16-year-old slave named Lincoln. Thirty years later, the same man was valued at £50.

To their owners, what mattered most was the slave's productivity. And slave-grown produce was exported from the plantations in ever growing volumes. Barrels of sugar and rum, tobacco, and later bales of cotton – all cultivated, processed and transported by enslaved peoples of the Americas – left the quaysides and harbours destined for the distilleries, refineries, warehouses and distributors of major European and North American ports and cities.

Transporting such goods to the ships was also slave work. Enslaved drivers and riders, draymen and wagoneers descended on quaysides across the Americas, supervising the transfer of produce from plantations to Atlantic ships. In ports, they mingled with town-dwelling slaves, including servants, skilled workers and transient

In fashionable 18th-century European society, black servants (sometimes enslaved) were a status symbol.

most visitors ignorant / what a surprise

sailors. Domestic slaves were everywhere. Visitors were often amazed by just how many slave servants worked and lived around the plantation 'Great Houses' (many of which were actually quite modest) or in their town houses. By the mid-18th century, black servants were even commonplace in fashionable Europe: African faces appear in numerous aristocratic family portraits. By then, the form of slavery created in the Americas had moved far beyond the confines of its plantation birthplace and could be found in the most unexpected places. There were slave cowboys on the American frontiers and slave domestics in Europe, although the legality of slavery in Europe remained uncertain and was increasingly challenged in local courts.

However, it was on the African coast and throughout the Americas that slavery was ubiquitous and unavoidable. Its prime purpose was to provide enforced labour for the American plantations, labour that was not readily recruited from among the free or semi-free of Europe or among native Americans. Wherever slavery came to dominate a local economy (for instance, in the Caribbean in the 18th century or the American South after 1800), slaves could be found everywhere. They undertook most of the back-breaking work on the

William Ansah Sessarakoo, son of an African slave trader, was himself sold in Barbados but was later freed and lionized in London in 1749. He finally returned home to Ghana.

Slaves and their descendants could be found in all corners of the Americas. This African-American cowboy was photographed in Kansas in the late 1870s.

plantations as well as ancillary and related tasks around those plantations. They worked in towns and ports throughout the Americas. They could be found on the American frontiers and even on the ships criss-crossing the Atlantic. Growing numbers of slaves, especially when baptized, became literate and devout Christians. Some managed to make remarkable strides in self-improvement and we know of notable examples of slaves who prospered, whose material lives seem remarkable for people who were themselves commodities. Olaudah Equiano, an ex-slave who rose to prominence in Britain in the decade 1787–97, left assets worth £1,000 when he died. However, such stories, important and revealing as they are, cannot erase the very different core reality of African slavery in the Americas. Millions of Africans found themselves cast ashore, thousands of miles from home, after enduring months of protracted misery, simply to work at strenuous and unrewarded work for a lifetime. They then bequeathed their bondage to their offspring born in the Americas, with slavery passing from mother to child.

Thanks to their work, the Americas were transformed. Even the landscape changed. The newly settled regions looked different, with swathes of land rendered fertile and profitable thanks to the sweat of African slaves. Yet the profits and rewards of those labours were to be found elsewhere. Whatever improvements slaves enjoyed in their lives, these were mere crumbs under the table: the feast was enjoyed by others, many of them out of sight on the far side of the Atlantic.

All the trappings of successful 18th-century commerce based on slavery are portrayed here: domestic happiness, a country house and a black servant.

ran away at all points they could
got off slave ships
tried to get weapons & kill the crew
using objects as bludgeons or weapons

more diversity after disembarking

ran away whenever possible, something to level one
escaped slaves used guerilla warfare
as main order
open revolts are much rarer
Sugar plantations had fewer, were
elevated bosses to revolt against then the Americas
revolts could get huuuuge
slaves used rumours to intimidate,
and Christianity to define themselves
as people and to unite blacks
slaves sand buzzed to make it easier

Slave Resistance

Africans resisted their bondage throughout the history of slavery. Slave owners everywhere lived in fear of slave resistance, especially slave revolt. Their worries were most acute on the slave ships. Indeed the very design and daily regime of the vessels revolved around the problems posed by African resistance. The ships' chains and guns offered ample proof that enslaved Africans might rebel at any moment. Nets were slung around the ships to stop Africans flinging themselves overboard (though many succeeded). But this was only the most extreme example of a theme that haunts the story of Atlantic slavery. Africans resisted their bondage as best they could, from the moment of enslavement through to life on the plantations. The slavery they endured was characterized throughout by violence, and Africans often responded with aggression of their own. But it would be wrong to think of slave resistance as merely a brutal reaction, for it often took complex and sometimes subtle, less noticeable forms. This is not surprising: slaves have rebelled and resisted in all other slave societies (the famous Spartacus revolt threatened Rome itself in 74 BC, and left 6,000 slaves crucified along the Appian Way). It now seems clear that African resistance was as important to the story of Atlantic slavery as the ascendancy of the slave owners.

Resistance took a host of forms and stemmed from a range of motives. Africans resisted enslavement from the moment they were first captured. Given the opportunity, they ran away from their captors on the trek towards the Atlantic coast, though escape became more difficult, more daunting, the further they were removed from

OPPOSITE Brutal revenge: settling old scores in the slave revolt in St Domingue (Haiti) in the 1790s.

M.Rainsford del.   Barlow sculp.

Revenge taken by the Black Army for the Cruelties practised

on them by the French.

Death of Capt. Ferrer, the Captain of the Amistad, July, 1839.

Don Jose Ruiz and Don Pedro Montez, of the Island of Cuba, having purchased fifty-three slaves at Havana, recently imported from Africa, put ther on board the Amistad, Capt. Ferrer, in order to transport them to Principe, another port on the Island of Cuba. After being out from Havana abou four days, the African captives on board, in order to obtain their freedom, and return to Africa, armed themselves with cane knives, and rose upon th Captain and crew of the vessel. Capt. Ferrer and the cook of the vessel were killed; two of the crew escaped; Ruiz and Montez were made prisoner.

Slave revolt on the *Amistad* and the death of Capt. Ferrer, 1839.

their own communities. It was no easy matter simply to run away and survive in a hostile environment, whether in Africa or the Americas.

Africans often tried to escape from the slave ships, especially when the vessel was at anchor for months off the African coast. Some hoped to get away and return home. Many of course were despondent at what had happened to them, and ship captains and surgeons paid close attention to signs of depression among the Africans they bought. They were keen to avoid buying slaves who were suicidal or unhealthy. Time and again, slave captains were warned by the ships' owners to take all possible measures against slave suicides: African deaths were clearly a financial loss. Despairing Africans were likely to fling themselves overboard, sometimes in a group but more often alone. Even the most resilient must have found life on the slave ships unbearable, and many simply wanted to put an end to it all by killing themselves.

These Mutinies are generally occasioned by the Sailors ill usage of these poor people...it has been my principal Care, to have the Negroes on board my Ship kindly used...   William Snelgrave, slave captain, 1734[1]

Sailors on the slave ships lived in permanent fear of African revolt. About one ship in ten experienced some form of slave rebellion, and many more were nipped in the bud. Some ships were overwhelmed by insurgent slaves. Others were completely destroyed in a fury of insurrection or blown up in the fighting. Many more saw insurgents defeated after a close-run fight between rebel Africans and a terrified crew. Africans plotted below decks, often helped by women and boys who had greater freedom on board. Sometimes they managed to seize weapons, tools or equipment, but sometimes they simply swarmed at the crew in numbers: their aim was always to kill the crew. The shipboard regime evolved to prevent such insurrections.

Africans were always under close scrutiny, allowed out of shackles only in small groups for exercise or feeding on deck. Care was taken to monitor the activities of those Africans who had greater freedom on the ships and might pass on information or material help in a rebellious plot. The myriad tools of a working ship must always be accounted for – tools, pieces of metal and wood could all become dangerous weapons in the hands of a rebel. Alert to all such opportunities, the Africans also noticed when any of the sailors died, even though the dead were disposed of at night to avoid drawing attention to the diminishing numbers of crewmen.

If plots were uncovered (and in the fearful climate of a slave ship it was all too easy to see plots, even where none existed), the plotters faced death and punishment on a horrifying scale. Reprisals were carried out in front of other Africans. Along the coast, the captains of neighbouring slave ships brought Africans on deck to watch as rebels were executed, dismembered and their remains hoisted aloft or cast to the sharks. Africans were left in no doubt about what happened to unsuccessful rebels. Former slave captain John Newton had tortured suspects in the thumbscrews: 'a dreadful engine which…can give intolerable anguish'. He knew of another slave captain who 'studied, with no small attention, how to make death as excruciating as possible'.[2] Even so, the crew could never be sure their human cargo would not explode. Slave ships simmered with brooding African despair on the one hand and the crew's terrified anxiety on the other – and this atmosphere continued right across the Atlantic.

The wonder is that more slave ships did not erupt into open revolt – their brutal regime was largely effective. The African survivors then carried into their American bondage the haunting memories of a terrifying oceanic ordeal, laced with the threat of vio-

A fight to the death – a revolt on a slave ship was the nightmare of slave traders everywhere.

Ship Revolts

Accounts of slave revolts on the ships are plentiful and vividly convey the terror and violence. Sailors distrusted all their African captives. One captain was told, in 1734, 'You'll have the needful guard over your slaves, and put not too much Confidence in the Women nor Children lest they happen to be Instrumental to your being surprised which may be fatall.'[3] Africans turned anything they could get hold of into a weapon: guns, swords, knives, hammers, buckets, shovels, wood, shackles, even feeding bowls – anything to inflict damage and death on their oppressors. In return, the crew resorted to all kinds of violent action. They fired at the Africans, fought them hand-to-hand, poured boiling water and fat over them, blocked off the gratings and covers to suffocate them in the holds, threw pepper and gunpowder over them, fired into the holds through portholes – anything to suppress revolt.

Dramatic image of a rebellious African, who uses a piece of wooden equipment found on the ship in a bid to secure his freedom.

lence and punishment. They never forgot the experience, and their stories entered the folklore of later generations in the slave quarters of the Americas.

The Atlantic crossing left large numbers of African survivors seriously harmed. Some did not overcome the illnesses picked up on the crossing. Death rates among Africans in their early years in the Americas reflect the damage caused by the slave ships. The traumas and sicknesses of the crossing did not purge the Africans of their defiance, but now, in a totally new setting, that defiance took on a variety of different forms.

Once on the plantations, large numbers of slaves ran away from their owners. Sometimes they were simply fleeing the harshness of a particular master or job. Often they were running off towards someone, seeking a loved one in a distant location. Sometimes their owners even knew where they were heading. Local newspapers were peppered with advertisements for runaway slaves, often containing a wealth of information about their age and condition, languages and skills, appearance and even their probable destination. A Virginian runaway named Ayre, 'although from Africa, affects to pronounce the English language very fine, or rather to clip it'.[4] In 1780 Sambo, a very old Jamaican slave 'who pretends to be blind', ran off and 'is supposed to be harboured by his son…'[5] Ten years later 'Diligence alias Junk' left her Jamaican owner: 'she frequently travels to Colbeck's Estate (where she has a husband called Chester)'.[6]

Some, mainly young men, were regular runaways, returning (to an anticipated beating) time and again. Their exasperated owners described them, in plantation ledgers and advertisements, as 'incorrigible runaways'. Some slaves clearly were not deterred by the practical difficulties of surviving on the run or the inevitable punishment facing them on their return. There were also circumstances in which slave owners were more liable to tolerate runaways – when times were hard and food was short, or when work was slack (as it sometimes was in seasonal agricultural work), it might be no great loss if a slave ran away temporarily – providing he or she could be found and returned when required.

Where geography allowed, some runaway slaves managed to escape from bondage completely, developing new isolated communities of 'maroons' (meaning 'untamed', from the Spanish *cimarrón*).

An African runaway surviving in the jungle in Surinam.

These first emerged during the early days of Spanish settlement. In the wild, inaccessible interiors of Brazil, Surinam and Jamaica, runaways created their own distinct communities, out of reach of both the planters and the colonial powers. Living like guerrillas, they were usually viewed as a threat to the established order, especially when they welcomed fresh runaways to join them. The authorities would try to bring them to heel by force, and there were periodic conflicts. But the maroons could be difficult to engage and defeat, and sometimes the result was an uneasy truce.

Like the captains and their crews on slave ships, slave owners and their white managers in the Americas distrusted their slaves, and this distrust was well founded. Everyone knew that slaves resisted

Slaves have run away from their owners in every slave society. It is generally seen as a form of slave resistance, but it was also an individual response to particular conditions. In the Americas both men and women ran away, but young men were especially likely to take a chance. It was usually a lone response: slaves tended not to run away in groups, which were harder to hide. It was extremely risky and dangerous. How could runaways survive in a hostile environment, especially when they were being chased? And how could they confirm their identity – their right to be where they were – or prove their freedom, when confronted? Slaves could be stopped, questioned and seized wherever they travelled or fled. They therefore needed friends and sympathizers to help when they were escaping. Indeed, we know that many simply could not have escaped, even temporarily, without the shelter, food and comfort of other slaves en route. They might be alone, but they were dependent on others.

Advertisement seeking the return of slave runaways, Missouri, 1860.

$200 Reward!

Ranaway from the sub-scriber, living in Saline county, on the 4th inst., two Negro men, named Jim and Jack---each aged about 25 years.

Jim

is dish-faced; has sore eyes and bad teeth; is of a light black or brown color; speaks quick, is about 5 feet 7 inches high; had on when last seen, blue cotton pants, white shirt, white fulled coat and new custom-made boots.

Jack

had on the same kind of clothing with shoes, has a very small foot, wears perhaps a No. 6 shoe, and has heavy tacks in the heels; is about the same height and color of Jim. They are doubtless aiming for K. T.

A reward of $100 each will be given if taken outside of the State, or $50 each if taken in the State, outside of Saline county. **G. D. WILLIAMS,**

Spring Garden, P. O., Pettis county, Missouri.

Harrisonville, Mo., June 7th, 1860.

whenever the chance arose, and slave rebellion was the ultimate planter's nightmare. These fears were reflected in colonial slave laws, with their extreme punishments for slave revolt and violence. The initial spread of Christianity in the British Caribbean, the arrival of large groups of Muslim slaves in Brazil, the impact of revolutionary ideas in the French islands after 1789 – each could provide the spark and sustenance for a major upheaval.

Rebellions flared up periodically across the Caribbean and Brazil, although in North America they were much less common and severe. It was immensely dangerous to plan and organize a revolt, and suspects were grotesquely tortured and killed. Even so, desperate and vengeful slaves (especially Africans) sometimes took the risk, either without warning or in response to specific grievances, and were inevitably repressed with the most draconian measures.

But slave owners did not always need to resort to the law to intimidate their slaves. Both Africans and their local-born offspring

Communities of escaped slaves – maroons – plagued Jamaican planters throughout the 18th century, leading to insurgent wars (here in the 1790s) and eventual peace treaties.

learned what to expect if they transgressed. They also knew that punishment might come their way for no particular reason: capricious blows or 'stripes' from a master's whip became a commonplace of plantation life, as did the sexual attacks and demands on female slaves. No slave could ever feel safe from the threat of physical danger inflicted by settlers who distrusted Africans in general.

The fate of unsuccessful slave rebels: dismemberment and hangings in Demerara after the revolt of 1823.

In the evening I took a walk about the plantations. Eugene was whipped for running away and had the [bit] put on him. I said my prayers and had good health, good thoughts, and good humour, thanks be to God Almighty.
Diary of William Byrd, Virginia planter, 1709[7]

However, this background of mutual distrust varied between colonial societies. Not surprisingly, it seems to have been worst on sugar plantations, where the slaves greatly outnumbered the whites.

Image of the successful slave rebel: from St Domingue in the 1790s.

At Worthy Park Estate in Jamaica in the 1780s and 1790s, upwards of 500 slaves were controlled by fewer than ten white men. On North American tobacco plantations the numbers were more balanced, and black and white labourers often worked side by side. Indeed it was unusual in colonial North America, except in some rice-growing regions, for slaves to outnumber whites. But slaves greatly outnumbered their owners and masters in the Caribbean and Brazil. This simple fact – a preponderance of slaves – may explain why the punishments meted out by those regimes and the consequent slave reactions were fiercer than in North America. It may also explain why rebellion was more common in Brazil and the Caribbean than in North America: slaves could see more easily the potential for revolt.

However, planters everywhere feared slave revolts. Most plantations were situated in isolated places, far from the local militia and military forces, so the whites were very much on their own when revolts erupted. Although usually well-armed, they were not only greatly outnumbered but faced slaves who might be equipped with a dangerous array of tools: the bills, axes, hoes, knives and machetes normally used to hack away at foliage and undergrowth. It was by no means certain that the masters' superior firepower would carry the day if slaves revolted. In truth the plantations, especially in the sugar colonies, were tinder-dry and ready to catch fire. Brazil and the Caribbean islands were plagued by servile revolts, often prompted by local incidents. But wherever revolt erupted, it was suppressed with savagery. In the aftermath of a slave revolt, all slaves – including those who had not been involved – invariably suffered from the predictable white backlash. Though less frequent, less violent and less insurrectionary in North America, slave rebellions remained the permanent and inescapable nightmare of slave owners throughout the history of African slavery.

The most crucial of all slave revolts in the Americas took place in the French Caribbean colony of St Domingue in 1791 (called Haiti after 1804). St Domingue was a unique society with all the ingredients for instability. The population consisted of huge numbers of Africans, most of them recently arrived, with few of the moderating elements provided by a more settled slave community. It was also ruled as fiercely as any slave society in the Americas. The outcome was slave upheaval on a massive scale. Rebellious slaves defeated the

OPPOSITE William Blake's portrayal of the torture of a female slave in Surinam, published in 1796.

Memorial to slave emancipation in Haiti.

planters, the colonial French, and subsequently Spanish and British invading armies. It was a revolution that sent shock waves throughout the Atlantic world and unsettled slave owners everywhere. Refugees (black and white) fled from Haiti throughout the Caribbean and beyond, settling as far away as New Orleans and Charleston. Although it was the only slave revolt in the Americas that succeeded in toppling a government, it established an example showing that slaves could secure their own freedom, and Haiti became a symbol for slaves everywhere.

Brazil too experienced major slave revolts, especially in the wake of large importations of Africans in the early 19th century. The most important and dangerous to the planters was the Male Islamic revolt in 1835. The Male uprising was unusual in that it looked back to the Muslim world left behind in Africa as the aim of the upheaval and used the language of Islam rather than the language of the rights of man, as in Haiti. By comparison the threats of revolt in North America – even when violent – were relatively small in scale and easily contained. Nat Turner's revolt in Virginia in 1831, for example, led to only 55 deaths (though many more slaves died in reprisals). In the same period a string of major slave upheavals rocked the British islands, notably in Jamaica in 1831–32. Time and again such revolts were met with grim violence, and this repression – combined with widespread evidence that Africans were desperate to end their bondage – helped to turn European opinion against slavery. By the 1830s Europe had changed enormously, and an increasing number of people began to believe that slavery had deep ethical and religious flaws. In this different cultural climate, the inherent violence of slavery – both in slave revolts and planters' revenge – was a source of growing public outrage among outsiders.

The destruction of the Roehampton estate in the Jamaican slave revolt of January 1832, known as the 'Baptist War'.

Moravians were among the first Protestants to convert and baptize slaves, here in North America.

A North American planter and his family attend a church service (conducted by a black preacher) alongside their slaves.

Slave revolts on the ships and in the plantation colonies peppered the history of Atlantic slavery, although they nonetheless remained unusual. Most slaves were not involved in upheavals (though they may, at heart, have longed to see them succeed). Yet slave owners feared slaves in general and were always ready to imagine that slaves were plotting against them: by definition, slaves were rebellious people who could not be trusted. This was of course a self-fulfilling proposition, demanding unceasing vigilance, intrusive scrutiny and unbending severity. Not surprisingly then, slave plots abounded. Rumours swirled among slave owners about mysterious activities, pernicious disruption caused by their healers and the dangers posed by subversive or prominent slaves. Plots, misunderstood words and misinterpreted actions all fed the underlying anxiety among slave owners across the Americas.

This is not to deny that in the tropics there was a lot to worry about. Sudden death was common: inexplicable illness and troubling physical problems afflicted people without warning. It was always tempting to think that slaves might be responsible for poisoning food or for evil spirits conjuring up bad medicine and curses. Of course, when slaves were cornered and threatened, they often told their masters what they wanted to hear.

Many slave owners also distrusted preachers keen to convert their slaves to Christianity. The major missionaries among slaves in the Caribbean and North America were Nonconformists: Moravians, Baptists and Methodists. And though they were generally cautious not to provoke the slaves, impressing on them the need for obedience and loyalty to their masters, the slaves could draw their own conclusions. They learned of the prospects of redemption and that salvation awaited. More critically perhaps, there soon emerged new generations of black preachers: people from the slave ranks who spoke in ways outsiders could not. Biblical language and stories – of crossing the Jordan, of reaching the Promised Land – spoke to their earthly condition and gave a Christian meaning to their own enslaved lives. Armed with a Bible, access to a chapel and a slave preacher, slaves found themselves in a whole new social network and with an ideology beyond the control of the slave owners. Gradually slaves began to use these tools as a means of organizing and speaking out against their own bondage.

Simply to protect themselves, slaves had to learn to dissemble, to accommodate, to adapt, and these vital lessons were passed on to their offspring. Slaves knew how to get by, how to appear to do as they were told – but not to do so too industriously, and without attracting attention. Too much effort or industry, too close an attention to their work, did not serve them well: better to be thought lazy, stupid and uncomprehending. Time and again, slave owners assumed their slaves were slow or simply did not understand (especially if they did not speak the same language). As often as not, the slaves were merely shuffling through the day at a pace which suited them rather than their taskmasters. It was all part of slave accommodation to the hostile and dangerous world around them and, in its own way, it was an aspect of slave resistance to life's intolerable demands.

A pattern can be discerned across the world of Atlantic slavery, from the slave ships off the shore of Africa to the plantations on the American tropical frontiers. It was a pattern of slave resistance, ranging from explosive revolt to quiet, unspoken truculence and foot-dragging. The lives of most slaves were miserable and often grim, but through their resistance, in all its varied forms, they tried to transform or at least shape their lives into something more tolerable.

Illustration from a 19th-century children's book showing the oppressiveness of slave field work.

Chapter 6

Abolition

For centuries the slave trade and slavery went virtually unchallenged. Early concerns expressed by churchmen were effectively drowned out by the voices of commercial interests. Too many people benefited from the slave system for complaints to be heeded about the suffering it caused. In addition, Europeans were a long way from the centre of the slave trade. Although thousands of ships left European ports for the African coast, they soon disappeared over the horizon. Slaves on the ships and plantations were far removed from the gaze (or concerns) of most Europeans – out of sight and out of mind.

This was not true, of course, for those free people of the Americas who were confronted by slavery, often on an immediate and daily basis. For them, any doubts about the morality of slavery were complicated by fears that black freedom – or even discussion about it – would bring social upheaval. People living in slave colonies worried about the dangers rather than the ethics of slavery. Thus the Atlantic slave system continued to thrive, unquestioned on ethical or religious grounds. But this began to change in the late 18th century, when the Atlantic slave system came under increasing attack. The first assault was limited to the slave trade (considered the most vulnerable target) and was followed, a generation later, by growing criticism of slavery itself. It was a long slow process that differed from one slave society (and one colonial power) to another, and it took a century to complete. The campaign against the slave trade began in 1787 and American slavery was finally abolished in its last bastion, Brazil, in 1888.

OPPOSITE British justice and Britannia celebrate the abolition of the slave trade in 1807, but without any acknowledgment of the role played by Africans themselves.

The two distinct movements – for the abolition of the slave trade and the emancipation of the slaves – each had its own complex roots. It seems ironic that the critical campaign against the slave trade first emerged in Britain, and just when the British trade was at its height. Discussion first began to stir after 1776 in the political debate about rights and representation that swirled around the campaign for American independence. That in turn prompted arguments in Britain about the slave trade. Yet in the 1780s alone the British carried 300,000 Africans across the Atlantic.

The effective origins of abolition sentiment grew out of Quaker agitation on both sides of the Atlantic. The Society of Friends in Philadelphia, always in close contact with British Friends, drew on older traditions to develop an early case against the slave trade. Indeed, George Fox, founder of the movement, had opposed slavery itself as early as the 1670s, though the Quakers' collective concerns

Early Voices

Although there were earlier objections to slavery, criticism did not become significant until the mid-18th century. It emerged from a mix of new religious organizations – notably Nonconformist – and secular Enlightenment writing. But what transformed abolition from a minority discussion among philosophers and clerics was the profoundly changing context. In the increasingly urban and literate communities of North America and especially Britain, information and ideas about slavery spread from an intellectual elite to a wider constituency. Growing numbers of people were confronted with the reality of slavery and the slave ships through the authentic voices of experience: the testimony of slave ship sailors and others who had seen slavery at first hand. What they described – and documented – was deeply shocking. Thus, what had once been a minority viewpoint was transformed, very quickly, into a popular issue. Tens of thousands of free tracts and hundreds of crowded lectures won over a huge audience to the idea that slavery and the slave trade were an abomination – and ought to be ended.

James Ramsay (1733–89), ex-naval surgeon turned abolitionist cleric. The first-hand experience evident in his writing greatly influenced British opinion against the slave trade.

were not fully articulated until the mid-18th century. By then other voices of opposition, from Scottish and French Enlightenment writers, had begun to make themselves heard. Nonetheless, such critics remained very much an isolated minority until the writings of a Philadelphia Quaker, Anthony Benezet, helped to transform the abolition movement on both sides of the Atlantic. For example, Benezet was responsible for converting John Wesley to abolitionism, and Wesley's support swung the growing band of Methodists against the slave trade. Soon a wider community of British Nonconformists lined up against the trade, and chapels across Britain provided strong and influential support for the abolition campaign.

In England, seeds of doubt about slavery had already been sown in a campaign for full black freedom led by the scholar Granville Sharp. In 1769 he published a major attack, *Representation of the Injustice and Dangerous Tendency of Admitting the Least Claims of*

William Dillwyn (1743–1824), a Pennsylvania-born Quaker who studied with Anthony Benezet, greatly influenced British abolition.

Granville Sharp (1735–1813), unsung hero of the abolition movement. A self-taught lawyer and scholar who defended enslaved and wronged Africans through a series of English court cases, he was an inspiring force behind the antislavery campaign.

Private Property in the Persons of Men in England, which asserted:

> Thus it must appear, that the plea of private property in a Negro, as in a horse or a dog, is very insufficient and defective…the comparing of a man to a beast, at any rate, is unnatural and unjust; as well as the seizing, and detaining him as such, is dangerous to the pretended proprietors.[1]

From the mid-1780s onwards an increasingly urban, literate population found itself exposed to waves of abolitionist literature that flew off their presses. The question of the fate of slaves was thrown into sharp relief by the focus on North America: would the newly independent USA persist with the slave trade and slavery – or not?

American criticism of the slave trade became widespread in the last years of the 18th century, perhaps because North America no longer needed new Africans. The existing slave population was expanding quickly, so the US trade in the 19th century was internal and overland, not transatlantic. But the South still clung to plantation slavery, and within twenty years slavery had spread beyond its traditional roots in the Old South and expanded greatly into the new cotton states of the Deep South. Other slave societies in the Americas, notably in Brazil and in the British, French and Spanish Caribbean, continued to demand slaves from Africa.

Resolved 'That the Slave-Trade was both impolitic and unjust…[and that committee be formed] for procuring such information and evidence, and publishing the same, as may tend to the abolition of the Slave Trade…'
Minutes of the Society for Effecting the Abolition of the Slave Trade, 1787[2]

The political climate began to change with the founding of the British Abolition Society in 1787 and the rapid growth of abolition groups across Britain. They campaigned locally against the trade, agitating among all classes of society, and bombarded Parliament with petitions signed by tens of thousands of people. Britain was inundated with abolitionist tracts circulated by a movement that was orchestrated by a national network and supported by an effective lecturing system, led by Thomas Clarkson. William Wilberforce emerged as its spokesman in the House of Commons, and Parlia-

OPPOSITE Flamboyant image of the hero of Haitian independence, sometimes called the Black Napoleon: Toussaint L'Ouverture (1743–1803).

Toussaint Louverture.

M.Rainsford del.

J.Barlow sculp.

Published as the Act directs, July 1.st 1805, by Ja.s Cundee, Ivy Lane, Paternoster Row.

ment soon recognized that the mood of the British people had turned decisively against the slave trade, regardless of its material benefits. This early political progress was temporarily stalled by external events: the French Revolution, the slave uprising in Haiti and the subsequent British military disaster attempting to conquer the colony in the 1790s. Britain lost upwards of 40,000 men in a vain attempt to take Haiti from the French, defeated by the insurgent ex-slaves led by Toussaint L'Ouverture and by the ravages of tropical disease that raced through the British ranks.

What transformed the discussion of the slave trade was the rapidly growing awareness of the horrors of the slave ships. The testimony of the men who had sailed on those ships (especially former captains and surgeons) and their evidence of the brutal facts of death and suffering, combined with the graphic imagery produced by the abolition movement, shocked and persuaded the British people. Abolitionists managed to make the campaign against the slave trade a genuinely popular cause. Their opponents, the planters and slave

Anti-abolition propaganda showing Africans and whites together enjoying a break from the routines of slave labour in St Vincent, c. 1801.

traders, could find no effective way of resisting or countering these arguments, and Parliament and government found themselves out-flanked: public opinion was ahead of the lawmakers. It was soon apparent that the British slave trade would be ended – the only questions were when, and under what conditions.

Britain, by this time the dominant power in Atlantic slave trading, was the only nation in which the rise of a popular abolitionist campaign put critical pressure on Parliament and government. The British abolitionists enjoyed a unique blend of conditions that contributed to their success. The initial Quaker impetus provided a widespread, business-like and well-run organization that facilitated the swift emergence of a national movement. The Quaker literate tradition also made possible the publication of tens of thousands of propaganda tracts. The campaign was brilliantly managed by Thomas Clarkson, author of *Essay on the Slavery and Commerce of the Human Species* (1787). He wrote:

Thomas Clarkson (1760–1846), the mastermind behind popular abolition in Britain.

> If the slave trade were abolished...the slave would be better fed...his hours of labour would be reduced to fewer in the day...his person would be more secure...he would have the power of appeal...every spur, that could promote population, would be administered.[3]

Clarkson toured the country (covering 35,000 miles on horseback between 1787 and 1794), gathering first-hand accounts from men who had served on the slave ships and lecturing everywhere he went. He proved, using this empirical and irrefutable evidence, that the slave ships were abominably cruel. The slave traders and planters disputed the abolitionists' case, but their arguments were simply incredible. Abolitionist literature was based on the raw witness of the men from the slave ships – their own words – which boldly stated what they had seen and experienced.

Supporters of the slave trade had one basic argument, the economic case: how

Abolition motif ('Am I not a Woman and a Sister?') on a pin-cushion.

Heb. 13. 3.

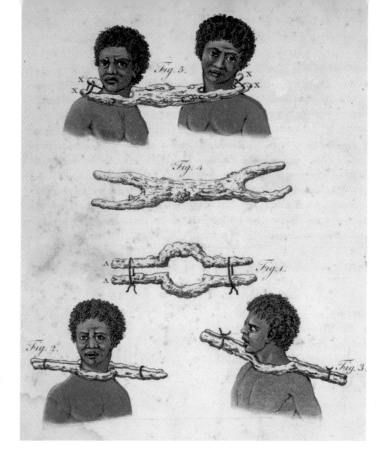

Illustrations from one of Thomas Clarkson's publications (1791), showing the harsh crudeness of enslavement on the African coast.

could the country contemplate abolition when so much prosperity continued to be generated by the Atlantic slave trade? But Clarkson had an answer to that: a sturdy chest packed with goods from Africa – pepper, cotton, timber, leather, dyes, textiles – all of which could form the basis for a more traditional trade with Africa. A lively, mutually beneficial 'normal' trade could thrive to and from Africa without resort to trading in humanity. This argument was later adopted by the best-known African in England, Olaudah Equiano, in his autobiography (1789) – a book which also became part of the abolitionist attack on the slave trade. Equiano was the most prominent of a group of Africans who played a role in the British abolition campaign, arguing a more fundamental case for black freedom. In 1788 he petitioned Queen Charlotte, wife of George III:

I do not solicit your royal pity for my own distress; my sufferings, although numerous, are in a measure forgotten. I supplicate your Majesty's compassion for millions of my African countrymen, who groan under the lash of tyranny in the West Indies.[4]

The growing popular awareness of African resistance to their sufferings, both on the ships and on the plantations, persuaded more

Olaudah Equiano (c. 1745–97), the African who spoke for the enslaved of Africa. His autobiography, self-published in 1789, was a critical contribution to the abolition campaign.

Sugar from the East Indies was not cultivated by slaves and thus became part of the abolitionist boycott of slave-grown produce.

Wedgwood's famous image of the kneeling slave, 'Am I not a man and a brother?', was reproduced in many different forms – including cameos, medallions and brooches – by abolitionists after 1787.

people to support the campaign against the British slave system. It was becoming clear beyond dispute that the Africans hated their bondage and wanted it ended.

The abolition movements in Britain and later in the USA were also unusual in attracting substantial female support. Women campaigned against the trade in a host of ways: through local abolition societies, publications and, particularly in the first phase, through the 'Anti-Saccarite' movement promoting the boycott of slave-grown sugar. Women were to prove even more prominent and influential in the later campaign against slavery itself from the 1820s onwards.

Abolitionists argued that ending the slave trade would force the Caribbean planters to treat their slaves better. Unable to buy new Africans, planters would only be able to increase the numbers of their slaves by ameliorating their conditions and thereby encouraging the slave population to grow normally. In fact, the reproductive problems of most slave populations were caused not so much by ill-treatment (though there was plenty of that) but by the peculiar demography of the slave colonies and the continuing health problems caused by the slave trade itself.

Abolitionists also employed two of the most effective political images ever used in a British political campaign. The kneeling, manacled slave asking 'Am I not a man and a brother?', first manufactured as a cameo brooch by the potter Josiah Wedgwood, became an instant icon. It has survived to this day as a graphic portrayal of the slave trade and the campaign against it. The other image was of the *Brookes* slave ship. Plans and cross-sections of the ship, with Africans crammed, sardine-like, head to toe, wherever there was space, struck a chord and remained in the public mind. These images suggesting teeming African humanity, trapped in an infernal seaborne hell, both horrified and persuaded those who saw them. Printed initially by Quakers in Plymouth, pictures of the *Brookes* were reproduced everywhere. If anyone needed to illustrate the horror of the slave ships, they had only to point to a picture of the *Brookes*.

These two images – the Wedgwood cameo and the *Brookes* – came to represent the entire abolitionist argument, graphically demonstrating the inhumanity of a system that kept Africans in chains and subjected to oceanic torment in British ships. They prompted a moral revulsion that no amount of economic self-

This wooden model of the slave ship Brookes *was used to great effect by William Wilberforce in the House of Commons to illustrate the terrible conditions on the slave ships.*

The British government had resisted the abolitionists' demands for many years, so – led by William Wilberforce – their plan was first to persuade Parliament to end the slave trade and then later slavery itself. At first the House of Commons was sympathetic (although the Lords proved resistant to the very end). But the French Revolution (1789), the slave revolt in Haiti (1791) and war with France (1793) set back the political campaign for abolition. Wilberforce persisted, though he was sometimes cast down by failures. In the end it took a change of government and the realignment of international fortunes, along with the sheer persistence of the abolitionists' efforts, before Parliament was finally won over to abolition in

1807. But historians continue to struggle with a basic question: how could the Atlantic's dominant slave trader turn its back on such a profitable business? The abolitionist cause was certainly swept along by a wave of public rhetoric, but there were also powerful visual images that both reflected and sustained the campaign. Josiah Wedgwood's plaque, showing a slave in chains on bended knee asking 'Am I not a man and a brother?', proved to be perhaps the most enduring icon. It captures, in the simplest and most easily digested form, the entire thrust of the abolition movement. Today, it makes for uncomfortable viewing: a supplicant African begging for what we would now consider to be his right. Yet it is hard to

overstate the impact of that image, reproduced in countless formats after 1787, in impressing and persuading a sceptical global public. Much the same is true of the graphic images of the *Brookes* slave ship: these also remained in the public mind as harrowing snapshots of the historical tragedy of the Atlantic slave trade. Although it is true that images of Africans in chains speak of African defeat and subjugation, they can also be interpreted differently: without the chains there could have been no slave trade, because African defiance and resistance were only subdued by such chains. Perhaps even more important, these were the images that ultimately helped to win over the public to the cause of abolition.

...be it therefore enacted...that from and after the 1st day of May 1807, the African slave trade...shall be...utterly abolished, prohibited and declared to be unlawful... Act of Parliament abolishing the slave trade, 1807[5]

interest could overcome. Thus it was that the ethical and religious arguments about the slave trade succeeded, within a relatively short period, in overcoming the vested interests of the slavers and their beneficiaries. The actual political process was complex, of course, and for a time overshadowed by war with France and revolution in Haiti. But the basic fact was indisputable: abolition swiftly out-flanked the slave lobby, gained the moral high ground and came to command a dominant political position.

Parliament was finally persuaded that the British slave trade should be ended in 1807, followed a year later by the Americans. The best remembered figure in this campaign is William Wilberforce, who was the critical force within Parliament, especially in arguing the case directly with his old friend, the Prime Minister, William Pitt. But the historical and popular concentration on Wilberforce and Parlia-

Parade through the town of Wootton Bassett, Wiltshire, in 1808, to celebrate the abolition of the slave trade.

ment has, over the years, distorted the real story of abolition. The end of the British slave trade was of course brought about by an Act of Parliament, but Parliament itself was won over not so much by what happened inside the legislative chambers as what went on outside in the country. Looking back, contemporaries generally agreed that Parliament had been slow to follow the overwhelming public mood in favour of abolition.

Idealized Brazilian coffee plantation, 1835.

The British and American legislation of 1807 and 1808 aimed to bring an end to a trade that had thrived for centuries, yet it left slavery in the Americas untouched. Slavery survived in the British colonies until 1838, and even then full emancipation only came when slave owners were compensated with £20 million by Parliament. Slavery – cotton slavery – boomed in the American South and was not ended until destroyed by the Civil War. Slavery also thrived in Cuba and Brazil, primarily on new coffee and tobacco plantations, which con-

William Wilberforce (1759–1833) in 1807.

Spañol.mira en el Plata.encadenas niun esclavo.
Su amargo llanto ceso. desde que Rosas humano.
De su Libertad ufano.compasivo y Generoso.
Prodigo este con presioso.al infeliz Africano.

MUERAN LOS SALBAGES UNITARIOS

RESTAURA

VIVA LA LIBERTAD

Libertad, no mas Tiranos

Las Esclavas de Bue. Air. Demuestran ser Libres y Gratas'a su Noble Libertador.

The Governor of Buenos Aires granting freedom to the slaves of the province.

tinued to import huge numbers of Africans despite the abolition laws and the efforts of the British and American navies. But eventually times began to change even in Cuba and Brazil, and political and economic opinion slowly turned against slavery. By mid-century, slavery was of dwindling importance and was finally outlawed in 1886 (Cuba) and 1888 (Brazil).

It was demand in the Americas up to the mid-19th century that encouraged the survival of the Atlantic slave trade after the abolition of 1807. Despite a British and American naval presence to intercept 'illicit' slave ships, and despite diplomatic pressure to cut off the supply of Africans through treaties with African leaders, more than 2.7 million Africans crossed the Atlantic in slave ships after 1807. The Atlantic trade did not die away until the 1860s, and by then most of the ships used the South Atlantic crossing between Angola and Brazil.

By the eve of the American Civil War, the dominant view on both sides of the Atlantic had turned firmly against slavery. Of course, many still found profit in slavery and it continued to have strong support, notably among planters, traders and their backers. But by 1860 slavery had become an anachronism in a Western world committed to a different philosophy of trade, business and politics.

Slavery proved more durable, however, more resistant to attack, in other regions of the world, notably in Africa and Asia. The overland slave trade across the Sahara and along the East African slave routes to Arabia and India continued throughout the 19th century and beyond, despite the European abolitionists and their legislation, navies and treaties.

Perhaps the most curious aspect of this entire story is that Britain, the country that dominated the Atlantic slave trade in the 18th century and seemed to benefit most from it, was the very country that turned its back on the trade and promptly re-invented itself as the world's leading abolitionist, trying to impose an end to the slave trade in all corners of the globe. The world's greatest poacher had become the world's most strident gamekeeper.

Boat from the Royal Navy ship HMS *London* chasing an Arab slave dhow near Zanzibar on the east coast of Africa in 1876–77, painted by the ship's chaplain.

Chapter 7

Legacies

The Atlantic slave trade ended long ago, yet it continues to cast a large and troubling shadow over the modern world. Indeed, few historical phenomena have had so durable and inescapable an influence over subsequent history. Some of the long-term legacies of Atlantic slavery are clearly visible, the most striking and permanent being the peopling of the Americas by Africans and their descendants. Today, numerous societies in the Caribbean and South America are overwhelmingly of African ancestry, but nowhere in the Americas has remained completely untouched by the enforced migration of Africans.

The consequences are not simply demographic: the slave heritage of millions in the Americas inevitably affects the way people view themselves and the world at large. As the historical facts of the slave trade have become more widely known, large numbers of people have become acutely aware that most traces of their ancestors disappeared in the brutal reality of the slave ships. They remain elusive in their anonymity: how is it possible to trace a family background when Africans landed in the Americas without names? And where in Africa did they come from originally?

The slave trade did more than remove millions of Africans from their homelands: it also removed their identities. Recent research has unearthed the names of 67,000 Africans from the slave ships (after 1819). But that figure is tiny compared to a total of 12 million people. A few exceptional Africans kept their own names, but the overwhelming majority were simply logged as numbers when they

OPPOSITE Anna Holmes, descendant of slaves, surveys an old slave dwelling – part of a tobacco plantation in the mid-19th century – newly restored and preserved in Maryland, 2005.

Population Changes

The migration of Europeans and Africans to the Americas had a damaging impact on the indigenous peoples of the hemisphere. The great empires of the Aztec, Maya and Inca collapsed (though the beginnings of their decline may have started earlier), and native populations everywhere were badly affected by diseases and illnesses to which they had little resistance. In the Caribbean, the native people largely disappeared. Taking their place, especially in the tropical colonies, were new populations of which the majority were usually black and enslaved while the minority were white and free. Later new groups emerged, born of the mixing of African, European and local indigenous people, who also made their presence felt. Under slavery, children inherited the slavery of their mother, but in time a free group of mixed-race people evolved. The terms used to describe them varied enormously. In Brazil a whole lexicon of categories evolved to describe every possible variant of racial mixing. People were ranked by origin and region, but above all by colour. The rule of thumb was simple (though its application was often tortuous): the darker the skin, the lower the status. Similar hierarchies arose in all the American slave societies. In the years immediately following slave emancipation in Jamaica, the island was home to about 16,000

whites, nearly 300,000 free black people and 68,000 so-called 'coloured' people. Racial mixing became commonplace throughout the colonial and post-imperial world, but its problematic resonance in slave societies often endured in the free communities that replaced them. And its legacy lives on.

A range of mixed-race people are pictured in a fashionable home in Martinique, 1775.

entered the slave ships. They were then renamed by their new owners in the Americas. Classical names such as Nero, Cato or Hannibal were popular, as were biblical names like Abraham and Isaac. Some reverted to an African name (Kofi, Quashi), while others were given an insulting name (Strumpet) or just a nickname (Billy). The African best known today as Olaudah Equiano had also been named Gustavus Vasa, Jacob and Michael. This confusion of naming and renaming served to strip away the individuality as well as the heritage of Africans, in effect robbing them of who they were.

Value £200: A Negro man named Abraham, about 26 years old, an exceeding good forge.

Slave sale advertisement, *Virginia Gazette*, 1768[1]

Not surprisingly then, people descended from slaves and seeking to know more about their ancestors have usually found themselves gazing into an anonymous past. As ever more people have become curious about their own family history, this anonymity of enslaved Africans has loomed large as a hurtful legacy. The search for African ancestry has become more insistent, especially in North America, since the 1970s (inspired especially by the remarkable impact of the US TV series *Roots*). More recently this search has been given a new twist by the growing sophistication in the use of DNA. Millions of people who had given up, who thought their African past had vanished in enslavement, have been given some hope of its recovery. Despite its current limitations, the potential of DNA is encouraging: allied to more traditional historical research, it has begun to yield compelling (though often emotionally complex) information about family origins. The fact that it might be possible to find a location, a region of origin, for enslaved Africans is an exciting development for people denied access to their family history. Science, in the form of DNA, might finally be able to restore the humanity of people who were long ago reduced to items of trade.

The use of African slave labour on the plantations of the Americas was designed to enrich its backers and major participants. Indeed, Atlantic slavery played an important role in generating wealth in the Western world. One group of beneficiaries, particularly

Make haste with the Sangaree, Quashie, and tell Quaco to drive the Birds up to me — I'm ready.

Caricature mocking the style and pretensions of British West Indian planters, published in 1807 after the abolition of the slave trade.

in the Americas, seems obvious enough: the successful planters (although there were also many who did not succeed). Their story was repeated from the Brazilian frontier to the US cotton states. At their most elaborate, planters' 'Great Houses' (many also owned town houses) were a physical reminder of their owners' wealth and status and their eagerness to display it. The more elaborate buildings, filled with the best of imported furnishings and luxuries, were usually positioned in an eye-catching spot overlooking the plantation, at a suitable distance away from the slaves. Such homes were the American equivalent of the fashionable retreats of Europe's rich and successful.

Yet planters everywhere led precarious personal and economic lives. Until quite late in the history of slavery they were reliant on outside suppliers of labour, and it was impossible to be certain about the quality of their crops or when those crops might reach world markets. The highly extended oceanic trade routes meant they were also at the mercy of weather and warfare. Even more important, planters were likely to be dependent on others – often very far away – for finance, credit and supplies.

It could take years from the planting of American crops such as sugar or tobacco until income was eventually received for them. Planters generally needed credit, especially for buying slaves, and that credit came from outside sources. It is true that local merchants and traders also lent money to planters, but their prime source of

Planters' Homes

The most successful and prosperous of planters, wherever they lived, built houses that reflected their wealth and aspirations. Today many of these have become tourist sites: architectural reminders of the riches that flowed from slavery. Indeed, many stately homes in Europe are evidence of the same story, established by families whose prosperity and status were created or secured either by trading in slaves and plantations or through successfully financing those who did. It is sometimes difficult to visualize the Africans when visiting such homes: too often their presence has been overshadowed by the modern emphasis on the picturesque. It is tempting to view these 'Great Houses' simply as beautiful buildings in glorious settings, yet they would not have existed without the enslaved labour of Africans.

Planters trying to ape the wealthy landed class in Britain: Rose Hall, Jamaica, a grand example of the Jamaican-Georgian style, built between 1750 and 1780.

Lloyd's Insurance building,
London, 1809.

capital lay outside the slave regions. They acquired money – but especially credit – from European merchants or, in the USA in the 19th century, from banks and merchants in the northern states. Planters in Barbados and Jamaica were thus indebted to merchants and bankers in Britain, while cotton planters in the South were financed by bankers in the cities of the North. The financial trail leads away from the plantations to the metropolitan heartlands: to New York City and Newport, Rhode Island, to London, Liverpool or Lisbon. The profit and loss of the Atlantic slave trade can therefore be calculated in those distant financial and commercial centres of the broader economy.

We know of numerous local merchants in Europe's major slave ports (Liverpool and Bordeaux, for example) who rose from modest origins to establish family fortunes and trading dynasties through investing in slave ships and plantations. They would often diversify their profits into banking and insurance before retiring to grand homes in the countryside. They also acted as bankers, extending credit to planters, in return for the Africans delivered by their ships. When the planters faced financial difficulties (when crops failed, for example, or commodity prices fell) the merchants would call in their debts and thereby become planters themselves. Merchants were thus transformed, first into bankers and then into planters. Some even moved into the highest strata of contemporary society. A spectacular example was the Lascelles family of Yorkshire. Originally farmers, then merchants, and later money-lenders to the planters, the Lascelles acquired Caribbean properties from indebted planters. Having become fabulously wealthy, the family was then ennobled, entering

I am sorry to observe that...the grand object of English navigators – indeed of all Christian navigators – is money-money-money... Letter from Ignatius Sancho, African critic of slavery, 1778[2]

the rarified world of the British aristocracy as the Harewoods of Harewood House. Others, much less vaunted, followed a similar pattern of investing in land and the grandeur of country homes or fashionable town houses: for example, the Longs of Fonthill and Jamaica, or the Pinneys of Bristol and St Kitts.

In truth, the wealth created by slavery was shared out in ways that are not always obvious. Financial institutions in 18th-century Britain and 19th-century USA – banks and insurance companies – invested in slave ships, plantations and slaving ventures. Indeed,

Harewood House, built between 1759 and 1771 for the Lascelles-Harewood family who were, by turns, Yorkshire farmers, London merchants and bankers, West Indian plantation owners, and finally elevated to the peerage.

Banner denouncing Negro apprenticeship as slavery under another name and inviting signatures to a petition to persuade Parliament to grant full freedom, c. 1835.

Slave owners were eventually compensated for the value of their emancipated slaves: the owner of 103 slaves on Good Intent plantation in British Guiana has completed the appropriate form to claim compensation from Parliament.

many other institutions also benefited from the slaving business. Major American universities (Yale and Brown, for example) profited from slavery. The Bank of England was active in slaving investments, and so too, in the 17th century, was the British monarchy.

At one level, it is no surprise that the major centres of trade to Africa and the Americas benefited from the prosperity generated by

[B]

CLAIM
FOR THE COMPENSATION TO BE AWARDED FOR SLAVES.

Name of Estate, or Domicile of Slaves. **BRITISH GUIANA.** No.

Good Intent District of Demerary & Essequebo.

THE CLAIM of *William King Esqr. of New Land & Threadneedle London as Exeutor of William Seaton, deced. - owner in fee of Plns. Good Intent* in the Parish of *St. John -*

By Geo. Warren his attorney

to the COMPENSATION for *One hundred and three* SLAVES in the possession of the said *William King -* on the 1st of August, 1834, duly registered, [except as undermentioned,] and described in the Return made thereof, on the   day of   1834.

Geo. Warren Jr.

Number of Slaves Registered 31st May, 1832......*One hundred and sixteen Slaves*

Alterations from 31st May, 1832, to 1st August, 1834.   116

INCREASE BY BIRTH.

Sex.	Name.	Age.	Mother's Name.	
Male	*Trim*	14 Month	*Rose*	
"	*Melville*	10 -	*Leonora*	2
				118

slaving. Equally, many of those working in senior positions on the slave ships and plantations – merchants, ships' officers, planters and colonial officials – returned to enjoy the rewards gained from slavery. A few made spectacular fortunes, but most received more modest returns. Even so, Atlantic slavery enabled untold numbers of Europeans and Americans to retire to an enviable and otherwise unattainable style of life.

The economics of slavery permeated American and European life. This was graphically revealed when slavery in the British colonies was finally ended, in 1834–38. Parliament emancipated British slaves by providing an astonishing £20 million to compensate the slave owners. In effect, Parliament was buying the slaves'

Gathering of slaves on the plantation of J. J. Smith near Beaufort, South Carolina, photographed by an official Civil War photographer in 1862 – the year of Lincoln's Emancipation Proclamation.

The miserable conditions endured by slaves seeking freedom in makeshift towns during and after emancipation: Slabtown, in the ruins of Hampton, Virginia.

freedom. This massive sum – about 40 per cent of the government's annual expenditure – was then allocated to all those with documented proof that they owned slaves. The bulk went, of course, to Caribbean property owners. But large numbers receiving compensation lived in Britain, including numerous residents of London, many of them successful and prominent people not known for their links to slavery. The ownership of slaves had, by the 1830s, become widely dispersed, especially through metropolitan British life. The same was true in the United States where, on the eve of the Civil War, 400,000 people owned slaves.

Clearly slavery did make some people very rich, and it also left large numbers very poor. Slavery and its aftermath spawned a vast and growing impoverished class without assets or resources. Throughout the Americas, from Brazil to the USA, the free black societies that emerged from local slavery were overwhelmingly poor. Although the last few decades have seen the rise of educated, successful and prosperous black communities in the Americas and more recently in Europe, this does not alter the simple point that slavery created vast wealth for a few and subsequently produced poverty, and often misery, for many more. However they tried, no matter how hard they worked or how far they migrated from the old 'house of bondage' to seek a new life for themselves, most ex-slaves and thei free descendants tended to remain mired in poverty.

Not only did ex-slaves inherit poverty, they also inherited cultural disdain from the outside world. Defenders of Atlantic slavery had made much of the idea that Africans were inferior to Europeans – even less than human – and of course as slaves they were legally regarded as commodities. But the slave system did not evolve and thrive because Africans were (or were viewed as) inferior: the selection of Africans in particular as slaves was a simple matter of economics. Africans were chosen as slaves primarily because they were cheap, could be acquired relatively easily on the African coast, and seemed available in abundance to replace dead slaves in the Americas. But slavery became much more than a profit-making economic institution. It also created a culture (embracing the law, politics and even common parlance) that expressed itself in racial terms. The most obvious distinguishing feature of Africans was their colour, and in the Western world, blackness has long held strong cultural significance, evoking dirt, sin, evil and baseness. In the complex and protracted evolution of Atlantic slavery, these deep-seated cultural values attached to blackness were incorporated into the

Grotesque and racist caricature of freed slaves after the American Civil War.

Cultural racism in the 1930s: a
French advertisement for soap.

George Cruikshank's caricature
of common racist stereotypes
at a London dining club, 1819.

evolving debate about slavery. Proponents of slavery drew upon the West's cultural antipathy to blackness to consign African humanity to a deeply inferior position. Although Atlantic slavery was born not of racial attitudes but of economics, these attitudes were nonetheless vital in supporting and maintaining African slavery – and they survived long after the slave systems themselves had disappeared. Stated simply, Atlantic slavery bequeathed to the modern world a toxic legacy of racial attitudes, some of which survive to the present day. The slave trade has cast a long and durable shadow.

Perhaps the most problematic consequence of slavery was its long-term impact on Africa itself. The brutal removal of so many people from their homelands inevitably wreaked huge damage and loss, generating waves of violence and disruption that swept across the affected regions. Yet there were clearly some African groups – elites, leaders, governors, trading dynasties – who benefited from the Atlantic trade. The imported goods – above all, firearms –exchanged for enslaved Africans served to enhance the status, prosperity and power of these African elites. Of course, this came at a terrible cost for

The NEW UNION CLUB.
Being a Representation of what took place at a celebrated Dinner, given by a celebrated _____ Society _____

the enslaved – and when the Atlantic slave trade ended, slavery within Africa was stronger and more pervasive than it had been before the Europeans arrived on the coast. Historians now broadly accept that the years of the Atlantic slave trade, from the 16th to the end of the 18th century, mark the period when Africa suffered stagnation. Some have argued that the Atlantic slaving presence, with all its devastating social and economic consequences for Africa, laid the basis for a broader under-development of Africa that has survived to this day.

Wherever we look – whether to Africa, the Americas or Europe – the consequences of the Atlantic slave trade were profound. It affected three continents for the best part of four centuries, and its consequences continue to disturb people on both sides of the Atlantic, often in ways we do not immediately recognize, down to the present day.

African refugees seeking safety on the border between Guinea and Sierra Leone, 2001.

Resources

Chronology

1447 Estimated 900 African slaves in Portugal

1471 Portuguese establish trading base at Elmina

1482 Portuguese build castle at Elmina

1490 Portuguese cultivate sugar in Sao Tome using African slaves

1553 Dutch begin to trade in African slaves

1562–63 Sir John Hawkins, first English slave trader, takes Africans to Hispaniola

1598–1637 Dutch, French and British establish slave forts in West Africa

1619 First African slaves are sold in Virginia

1625–55 British establish colonies in the Caribbean

1672 Royal African Company is founded to control British slave trade

1730–40 First Maroon War in Jamaica

1739 Stono Rebellion in South Carolina

1760 Tackey's Rebellion in Jamaica

1776–83 War of American Independence

1787 Society to Abolish the Slave Trade is founded in London

1789 French Revolution; 'Rights of Man'

1791 Slave uprising in St Domingue (Haiti)

1795–96 Second Maroon War in Jamaica

1795–97 Fedon's Rebellion in Grenada

1800 Gabriel Prosser Revolt in Virginia

1804 Independence of Republic of Haiti

1807–8 Slave trade is abolished by Britain and USA

1816 Slave rebellion in Barbados

1819 Royal Navy's anti-slave trade squadron is founded

1822 Denmark Vesey's Revolt in South Carolina

1823 Slave revolution in Demerara (Guyana)

1831 Nat Turner's Revolt in Virginia

1831–32 Baptist War: Jamaican slave revolt

1834 Slavery is replaced by apprenticeship in British colonies

1835 Male uprising

1838 Full freedom in British colonies

1861–65 American Civil War

1865 Thirteenth Amendment abolishes slavery in USA

1886 Slavery is abolished in Cuba

1888 Slavery is abolished in Brazil

Notes

Chapter 1 The European Slave Trade with Africa

1 Hunwick, John, 'Islamic Law and Polemics over Race and Slavery in North and West Africa (16th–19th century)', in Shaun E. Marmon (ed.), *Slavery in the Islamic Middle East* (Princeton: 1999), p. 54

2 Fisher, N. R. E., *Slavery in Classical Greece* (London: 1993), p. 73

Chapter 2 Sugar and Slavery

1 Donnan, Elizabeth, *Documents Illustrative of the History of the Slave Trade to America*, 4 vols (Washington, DC: 1930–35), I, pp. 41–42

2 Ibid, pp. 125–26

Chapter 3 The Middle Passage

1 'Evidence of James Penny', British Sessional Papers, Commons, Accounts and Papers, 1789, XXVI, Part 2

2 Donnan, Elizabeth, *Documents Illustrative of the History of the Slave Trade to America*, 4 vols (Washington, DC: 1930–35), I, p. 293

3 Atkins, John, *A Voyage to Guinea, Brasil and the West Indies* (London: 1735), p. 158

4 Bowes, Christopher, *Medical Log of the Slaver the 'Lord Stanley'*, 1792, Library of the Royal College of Surgeons, London

5 Donnan, *Documents*, I, p. 295

6 Falconbridge, Alexander, *Account of the Slave Trade on the Coast of Africa* (London: 1788), p. 25

Chapter 4 Destinations and Slave Life

1 Donnan, Elizabeth, *Documents Illustrative of the History of the Slave Trade to America*, 4 vols (Washington, DC: 1930–35), I, pp. 164–65

2 Jones, Hugh, *The Present State of Virginia* (London: 1724), p. 37

3 *Daily Advertiser*, Kingston, 7 June 1790

4 Morgan, Edmund S., *Virginians at Home* (Charlottesville, Virginia: 1952), pp. 51–54

Chapter 5 Slave Resistance

1 Snelgrave, William, *A New Account of Some Parts of Guinea* (London: 1734), p. 162
2 Newton, John, *The Journal of a Slave Trader*, eds Bernard Martin and Mark Spurrell (London: 1962), p. 77
3 Christopher, Emma, *Slave Ship Sailors and their Captive Cargoes, 1730–1807* (Cambridge: 2006), p. 183
4 Mullin, Michael (ed.), *American Negro Slavery: A Documentary History* (New York: 1976), p. 110
5 *Royal Gazette*, Kingston, 23 December 1780
6 *Daily Advertiser*, Kingston, 29 January 1790
7 Wright, Louis B. and Marion Tinling (eds), T*he Secret Diary of William Byrd of Westover, 1709–1721* (Richmond, Virginia: 1941), p. 46

Chapter 6 Abolition

1 Sharp, Granville, *Representation of the Injustice and Dangerous Tendency of Admitting the Least Claims of Private Property in the Persons of Men in England* (London: 1769), p. 15
2 Clarkson, Thomas, *The History of the Rise, Progress and Accomplishment of the Abolition of the Slave Trade by the British Parliament*, 2 vols (London: 1808), I, p. 255
3 Clarkson, Thomas, *Essay on the Impolicy of the African Slave Trade* (London: 1788), p. 100
4 Equiano, Olaudah, *The Interesting Narrative and Other Writings*, ed. Vincent Carretta (London: 1998), pp. 231–32
5 'Act for the Abolition of the Slave Trade, 1807', in A. Aspinall and E. Anthony Smith (eds), *English Historical Documents* (London: 1959), pp. 803–4

Chapter 7 Legacies

1 *Virginia Gazette*, 1 December 1768
2 *Letters of the Late Ignatius Sancho, an African in Two Volumes*, 1782, ed. Vincent Carretta (London: 1998), p. 130

Further Reading

Berlin, Ira, *Many Thousands Gone: The First Two Centuries of Slavery in North America* (Cambridge, Massachusetts: 1998)

Clarence-Smith, William Gervaise, *Islam and the Abolition of Slavery* (Oxford: 2006)

Davis, David Brion, *Inhuman Bondage: The Rise and Fall of Slavery in the New World* (New York: 2006)

Drescher, Seymour, *Abolition: A History of Slavery and Anti-Slavery* (Cambridge: 2009)

Eltis, David, *The Rise of African Slavery in the Americas* (Cambridge: 2000)

Heuman, Gad and James Walvin (eds), *The Slavery Reader* (London: 2003)

Inikori, Joseph I., *Africans and Industrial Revolution: A Study in International Trade and Economic Development* (Cambridge: 2002)

Morgan, Kenneth, *Slavery and the British Empire: From Africa to America* (Oxford: 2007)

Richardson, David, Suzanne Schwarz and Anthony Tibbles (eds), *Liverpool and Transatlantic Slavery* (Liverpool: 2007)

Walvin, James, *An Atlas of Slavery* (London: 2006)

Translations and Transcriptions of the Documents

1 List of goods for the purchase of slaves ('Lijst van goederen voor de inkoop van slaven') for a Dutch slaving voyage, 1688.

> Form of current and for your honoured Company most profitable trades necessary for the speedy acquisition of slaves in Offra and Ardra. Done 14 August 1688
>
> 16,500 cowry shells
> 8,000 flat dishes with broad rims
> 80 assorted flat copper saucers
> 200 serviettes
> 40 platilios [type of linen]
> 200 graaten [probably beads made from bone]
> 30 white Guinees lijnwaet [pieces of textile]
> 60 fine meurizoen [probably a type of textile]
> 10 pieces of decorated silk from Haarlem
> 8 fine coral
> 10 red damask
> 5,000 turquoise beads of which a sample is included below
> 500 white quispel [beads]
> 500 iron bars
> 12 guns, half copper, half iron
> 500 gunpowder
> 10 half amen French brandy [amen = a measure]
> 2 celders of 150 stoops bottles of fine distilled waters [celder and stoop = measures]
>
> Additionally, Van Hoolwerff asks for glassware such as small beer glasses and engraved rummers.

2 Pages from the log of the Liverpool slave ship *Unity*, captained by Robert Norris, on a voyage to Calabar via Holland, 1769–70. Noted along with his routine observations of wind speed, weather and the number of barrels of water they have used are details of an attempted

slave rebellion, ending with this comment: 'Their obstinacy put me under the necessity of shooting the ringleader'.

3 Newspaper cutting in which rewards for runaway slaves appear alongside those for missing horses, from the Kingston (Jamaica) *Mercury*, July/August 1779. Each advertisement describes the slave's personal characteristics – origin, age, name, health, trade – and suggests where he might be found. Such sources provide important evidence for reconstructing the lives of 18th-century slaves.

4 Letter dated 1783 from an African to his Liverpool shipping contact, which offers a revealing insight into relations between African and European slave traders. The African, Egboyoung Offeong, specifies precisely which goods he wants from Liverpool, to be exchanged for Africans, and informs his British partners of the progress of a recently arrived slave ship. Offeong concludes by hoping for an end to military conflict: the previous seven years had been dominated by the War of American Independence, with disruptive consequences all the way to the African slave coast.

> Dear Gentlemen / Sir, / Captain
>
> John Burrow arrived at this river on the fourth day of May with a very fine cargo, only we want more iron bar and romalles [cloth] and powder and ordnance and shot as them be finest thing for our trade as we will send Captain Burrow away with 450 or 460 slaves after October. I hope his ships carry 450 or 460 slaves and I hope he will send by tender 340 or 330 slaves. I think so, as you may, get the cargo ready before he come home. I don't keep him long and I think he'll get to Liverpool 15 or 20 day March – Mind send very little salt and mugs as you may. Send round white and round green and round yellow bead for money, salt and mugs. I wish no more war for England.
>
> I am your dear Egboyoung Offeong
> Old Calabar, July 23rd 1783

5 Handwritten minutes of the establishment of the Committee for Abolition of the Slave-Trade, London, 22 May 1787, listing the names of the twelve founding members.

May 22 1787

At a meeting held for the Purpose of taking the Slave Trade into Consideration, it was resolved that the said Trade was both impolitick and unjust.

Resolved, that Granville Sharpe, Joseph Woods, Samuel Hoare junior, William Dillwyn, George Harrison, James Phillips, Richard Phillips, Thomas Clarkson, Philip Sansom, John Lloyd, Joseph Hooper and John Barton be a Committee for procuring such Information and Evidence, and for distributing Clarkson's Essay and such other Publications, as may tend to the Abolition of the Slave-Trade, and for directing the application of such monies, as are already, or may hereafter be collected, for the above Purposes.

Resolved, that three Members be a Quorum.

Resolved, that Samuel Hoare junior be appointed Treasurer to the Society.

Resolved, that the Treasurer pay no money on account of this Society, but by Order of the Committee.

Resolved, that one hundred copies of these Resolutions be printed, with this addition, viz. The Subscriptions of such, as are disposed to contribute towards carrying on the Design of this Institution, will be received by the Treasurer, or any member of the Committee.

Adjourned to Thursday Evening May the 24th at six o'clock.

6 Stowage of the British slave ship *Brookes* under the Regulated Slave Trade Act of 1788.

Note: The "Brookes," after the Regulation Act of 1788, was allowed to carry 454 Slaves. She could stow this number by following the rule adopted in this plate namely of allowing a space of 6 Ft by 1 Ft 4 In to each man; 5 Ft 10 In by 1 Ft 4 In to each woman, & 5 Ft by 1 Ft 2 In to each boy, but so much space as this was seldom allowed even after the Regulation Act. It was proved by the confession of the Slave Merchant that before the above Act the Brookes had at one time carried as many as 609 Slaves. This was done by taking some out of Irons & locking them spoonwise (to use the technical term) that is by stowing one within the distended legs of the other.

Fig 1 Longitudinal Section

Fig 2 Plan of lower deck with the stowage of 292 slaves, 130 of these being stowed under the shelves as shewn in figure 3 & figure 5.

Fig 3 Plan shewing the stowage of 130 additional slaves round the wings or sides of the lower deck by means of platforms or shelves (in the manner of galleries in a church) the slaves stowed on the shelves and below them have only a height of 2 feet 7 inches between the beams and far less under the beams. See Fig. 1.

Fig 4 Cross Section at the Poop

Fig 5 Cross Section amidships

Fig 6 Lower tier of Slaves under the Poop

Fig 7 Shelf tier of Slaves under the Poop

7 Remarkable letter revealing an attempt by a literate North American slave, Edward George Codrington, to purchase his freedom, promising to continue to work for his master as a skilled farrier.

> Cotton N Work Estate Sep 6th
>
> My Dear Master
>
> I have taken the liberty of addressing you on a most particular favor, that is asking your permission to allow me the privilege of purchasing myself and I hope this may not be an offence to you if so I will be extremely sorry my dear master this address is with a sincere regard toward your welfare as well as myself I shiver at the attempt of asking the favor from knowing that you have a family which must inherit us hereafter but I trust in your kindness with god willing that this letter should reach you and also meeting you in good health and my young master and the other part of the family my dear master I do not ask this favor for any other purpose than for the benefit of myself nor shall I shrink from the profession that I now hold as a farrier it is never my intention if I was three times free to give up that name of CBC therefore I will if you will be kind enough to grant me this favor bind myself down to serve you in the farrier line I have not waited on mr. Jarritt who is our present attorney who I know would be willing to lead me through any thing that is legal but it was impossible for me to do so when I knew his mind must been sick from the abusive treatment that he has received from a few of Betty's hope and the garden's negroes in the behalf of you
>
> I remain my Dear master your most Humble and Obedient Servant
> Edward George Codrington

8 Notice of a slave sale by court order, Charleston, 11 January 1859, specifying the ages and names of the slaves and the purchase terms. The scribbled marginal notes, perhaps from a prospective buyer, comment on their physical condition and qualities.

9 Lithograph illustrating Abraham Lincoln's 1862 Emancipation Proclamation with scenes of slavery and freedom. But freedom was only fully confirmed by the Thirteenth Amendment to the United States Constitution after the Civil War ended in 1865.

Emancipation Proclamation

Whereas, on the 22nd day of September in the year of our Lord 1862 a Proclamation was issued by the President of the United States containing among other things the following, to wit:

That on the first day of January, in the year of our Lord 1863 all persons held as slaves within any State or designated part of a State the people whereof shall then be in rebellion against the United States, shall be then thenceforward and forever free; and the Executive Government of the United States, including the military and naval authority thereof, will recognize and maintain the freedom of such persons, and will do no act or acts to repress such persons or any of them in any efforts they may make for their actual freedom. That the Executive will, on the first day of January aforesaid, by proclamation, designate the States and parts of States, if any, in which the people thereof, respectively, shall then be in rebellion against the United States; and the fact that any State, or the people thereof, shall on that day be, in good faith, represented in the Congress of the United States by members chosen thereto at elections wherein a majority of the qualified voters of such State shall have participated, shall, in the absence of strong countervailing testimony, be deemed conclusive evidence that such State and the people thereof are not then in rebellion against the United States.

Now, therefore I, Abraham Lincoln, President of the United States, by virtue of the power in me vested as Commander-in-Chief of the Army and Navy in time of actual armed rebellion against the authority and government of the United States, and as a fit and necessary war measure for suppressing said rebellion, do, on this first day of January, in the year of our Lord one thousand eight hundred and sixty-three, and in accordance with my purpose so to do publicly proclaimed for the full period of one hundred days, from the day first above mentioned, order and designate as the States and parts of States wherein the people thereof respectively, are this day in rebellion against the United States, the following, to wit Arkansas, Texas, Louisiana – except the Parishes of St. Bernard, Plaquemines, Jefferson, St. John, St. Charles, St. James Ascension, Assumption, Terre Bonne, Lafourche, St. Mary, St. Martin, and Orleans, including the City of New Orleans – Mississippi, Alabama, Florida, Georgia, South Carolina, North Carolina, and Virginia – except the forty eight counties designated as West Virginia, and also the counties of Berkley, Accomac, Northampton, Elizabeth City, York, Princess Ann, and Norfolk, including the cities of Norfolk and Portsmouth, and which excepted parts, are for the present, left precisely as if this proclamation were not issued. And by virtue of the power and for the purpose aforesaid, I do order and declare that all persons held as slaves within said designated States and parts of States are and henceforward shall be free; and that the executive government of the United States, including the military and naval authorities thereof, will recognize and maintain the freedom of said persons. And I hereby enjoin upon the people so declared to be free to abstain from all violence, unless in necessary self-defense, and I recommend to them that, in all cases when allowed, they labor faithfully for reasonable wages.

And I further declare and make known, that such persons of suitable condition, will be received into the armed service of the United States to garrison forts, positions, stations, and other places, and to man vessels of all sorts in said service.

And upon this, sincerely believed to be an act of justice, warranted by the Constitution, upon military necessity, I invoke the considerate judgment of mankind and the gracious favor of Almighty God.

In witness whereof, I have hereunto set my hand and caused the seal of the United States to be affixed.

Done at the City of Washington, this first day of January, in the year of our Lord one thousand eight hundred and sixty three, and of the Independence of the United States of America the eighty seventh.

A. Lincoln

10 The formal legal announcement of the emancipation of Brazilian slaves: Lei Aurea (The Golden Law), 13 May 1888. The Lei Aurea had just two articles — Article 1: From this date, slavery is declared abolished in Brazil; and Article 2: All dispositions to the contrary are revoked. By this time slavery had already ended throughout the Americas, and slaves were simply slipping away. In fact, Brazilian slavery had been dying out long before full freedom came: it no longer made economic or political sense, and this document only confirmed the inevitable.

Sources of Illustrations

akg-images 122; British Library/akg-images 6, 14, 43, 46, 72, 73, 77, 92, 95; André Held/akg-images 27ar; World History Archive/Alamy 99; from d'Alembert, J. and Diderot, D. (eds), *L'Encyclopédie ou Dictionnaire raisonné des lettres, des sciences et des arts* (Paris 1751–72) 71; from de Amorim Castro, J., *Treatise on the species of tobacco cultivated in Brazil* (1792) 64; Gianni Dagli Orti/Maritime Museum, Kronborg Castle, Denmark/The Art Archive 42; Gianni Dagli Orti/Science Academy, Lisbon/The Art Archive 21; Gianni Dagli Orti/Bibliothèque des Art Décoratifs, Paris/The Art Archive 13b; Gianni Dagli Orti/Musée du Louvre, Paris/The Art Archive 32, 38; Gianni Dagli Orti/Private Collection/The Art Archive 13a; Gianni Dagli Orti/Biblioteca National do Rio de Janeiro, Brazil/The Art Archive 66; Eileen Tweedy/The Art Archive 112; V&A Images/Victoria and Albert Museum, London/The Art Archive 7, 30a; Museu de Ceràmica, Barcelona 48; from Benzoni, G., *Americae pars quarta* (Frankfurt a.M., J. Feyerbend, for Theodor de Bry 1594) 37b; from Biard, F., *Deux Années au Brésil* (Paris 1862) 65; from Branagan, T., *The Penitential Tyrant* (Samuel Wood, New York 1807) 60; Michael Graham-Stewart/Bridgeman Art Library 50–1, 61; Harewood House Trust/Bridgeman Art Library 123; Wilberforce House, Hull City Museums and Art Galleries/Bridgeman Art Library 111; Academia das Ciencias de Lisboa, Lisbon/Giraudon/Bridgeman Art Library 25; University of Liverpool Art Gallery & Collections/Bridgeman Art Library 47; Yale Center for British Art, Paul Mellon Collection/Bridgeman Art Library 81a; Bibliothèque Nationale, Paris/Giraudon/Bridgeman Art Library 28–29; American Antiquarian Society, Worcester, Massachusetts/Bridgeman Art Library 62; Bristol City Museum and Art Gallery 49b; National Library of Australia, Canberra (nla.pic-an8934776) 2–3; from Chambon, M., *Le commerce de l'Amerique par Marseille* (1764) 34a; from Clarkson, T., *Letters on the slave trade...* (London 1791) 108; © Bernd Kohlhas/Corbis 121; © Patrick Robert/Corbis Sygma 129; from Dalzel, A., *A History of Dahomey* (London 1793) 30b; from Debret, J. B., *Voyage Pittoresque dans le Brésil* (1835) 113a; from Dioscurides, *Tractatus de herbis* (France, 15th century) 33; from Dufour, P. S., *Traites Nouveaux & Curieux du Café, du Thé et du Chocolat* (The Hague 1671) 36b; Wallace Collection, London/Werner Forman Archive 27al; Win McNamee/Getty Images 117; Veronique de Viguerie/Getty Images 19; Nationaal Archief, The Hague, Aanwinsten Collectie Afdeling Kaarten en Tekeningen (nummer toegang 4.AANW, inv. nr. 1569 40b); *Harper's Weekly* (1860s) 126, 127;

from *Histoire générale des drogues* (Paris 1694) 36a; from *Histoire Générale des Voyages, ou Nouvelle Collection de toutes les relations de voyages par mer et par terre*, part VI (Paris 1747) 53b; The Menil Collection, Houston 81b; Wilberforce Museum, Hull City Museums and Art Galleries 124r; Iberfoto/photoaisa 114; from *The Illustrated London News* (Nov. 29, 1856) 69; Kansas State Historical Society 82, 91; Courtesy National Library of Jamaica, Kingston 97; from *Kurze Zuverässige Nachricht* (1757) 98a; from Laporte, A., *Récits de vieux marins* (Paris 1883) 87; Merseyside Maritime Museum, National Museums Liverpool 49a; Courtesy of Anti-Slavery International, London 124l; British Library, London 20, 22, 44 (Add. Ms. 43379A), 93 (8157.bb.9.1); British Museum, London 24, 26b, 39, 80, 110a; Trustees of the British Museum, London 35; Museum of London 83; National Maritime Museum, London 4–5, 9, 15, 16, 31, 40a, 53a, 54a, 54b, 55, 58, 59, 79, 100, 106, 107a, 107b, 109, 110b, 113b, 115, 120, 128b; National Portrait Gallery, London 17, 102, 103b; Library of the Religious Society of Friends, London 103a; Royal Commonwealth Society, London 41; Wellcome Library, London 90; Museo de América, Madrid 45; Biblioteca Estense Universitaria, Modena, Courtesy Ministry of Heritage and Culture 8; The Historic New Orleans Collection (accession no. 1975.93.3-4) 74–75; Photographs and Prints Division, Schomburg Center for Research in Black Culture, The New York Public Library, Astor, Lenox and Tilden Foundations 68; from Smith, W., *Thirty different drafts of Guinea* (London c. 1727), Courtesy The Mariners' Museum, Newport News, Virginia 34b; Bibliothèque Forney, Paris 128a; Bibliothèque Nationale, Paris 12, 23; Ministère de l'Outre-Mer, Paris 118; from Rainsford, M., *An Historical Account of the Black Empire of Hayti...* (London 1805) 85, 96, 105; White Images/Scala, Florence 11, 88; Museo de Bellas Artes, Seville 37a; Iris & B. Gerald Cantor Center for Visual Art, Stanford University Committee for Art Acquisitions Fund 94; Royal Museum for Central Africa, Tervuren 26a; from Walsh, F. R., *Notices of Brazil*, vol. II (London 1830) 52; Library of Congress, Washington, DC 1, 56, 78l, 78r, 86, 125

Facsimile documents British Library/akg-images 5; Gianni Dagli Orti/Museu Historico Nacional, Rio de Janeiro, Brazil/The Art Archive 10; Michael Graham-Stewart/Bridgeman Art Library 8; Nationaal Archief, The Hague, Tweede West-Indische Compagnie (nummer toegang 1.05.01.02, inv. nr. 180) 1; Merseyside Maritime Museum, National Museums Liverpool 2; Library of Congress, Washington, DC 6, 9; Courtesy Wisbech and Fenland Museum 4

Index

Page numbers in *italic* refer to illustrations